CREATIVE COLOR

An Analysis and Synthesis

of

Useful Color Knowledge

Compiled, Written, Edited and Published
by
The Essene Fellowship of Peace
Hemet, California

PUBLISHER'S DISCLAIMER

This book is not meant to replace the services of a physician nor is it intended as a substitute for personal medical care.

All rights reserved. No part of this book may be reproduced by any mechanical, photographic or electronic process, or in the form of a phonograph recording, compact disc or cassette tape recording, nor may it be stored in a retrieval system, transmitted, translated into another language, or otherwise copied for public or private use, excepting brief passages for purposes of review, without the permission of the publisher, except as indicated on page 111.

This book incorporates the Original Course in Creative Color Analysis, by Mary Dies Weddell, as taught and illustrated by Miriam B. Willis.

Copyright to Illustrations assigned by Miriam B. Willis and Constance E. Smith to the Spiritual Church of Ataraxia, Inc. 1984.

Permission was given to publish excerpts from the writings of Mary D. Weddell, George W. Weddell, M.D. and from Miriam B. Willis.

This logo, suggestive of the infinity sign, symbolizes the flow of knowledge received from higher dimensions, given to the individual, and through the individual to the world. By joining the two halves — the two dimensions of knowledge — the endless circle of God's love, of creation itself, is formed.

Cover design by Esther S. Barnes.

First Edition
Copyright 1988
Spiritual Church of Ataraxia, Inc., The Essene Fellowship of Peace
Post Office Box 5242, Hemet, California 92344

Library of Congress Catalog Card Number: 88-81957

ISBN: 0-9620292-0-3

Printed in the United States of America by the Franklin Press,
1001 S. Arrowhead Avenue, San Bernardino, California 92408

DEDICATION

In appreciation of the gifts of color knowledge

given by

Mary Dies Weddell

George W. Weddell

Miriam B. Willis

This book is lovingly dedicated to those

seekers who receive and to those who seek

to give the higher spiritual truths for

the benefit of all mankind.

CONTENTS

Dedication

List of Illustrations

Publisher's Preface

Acknowledgments

Introduction

Mary's Challenge and Philosophy

Chapter

    1. BIOGRAPHICAL BACKGROUND 1

        Mary D. Weddell
        George W. Weddell, M.D.
        Miriam B. Willis

    2. COLOR AND MAN 17

        What Color Is
        The Aura
        The Inner Channel

    3. CORE OF COLOR KNOWLEDGE 61

        Original definitions, color descriptions and
           illustrations of the Color Rays 62

        Original definitions and color descriptions of
           the Basic Arc of Purple 63

        Color descriptions and meanings of the
           Psychological Arcs 65

Expanded meanings of the Color Rays

    Psychological Arcs of Green, Blue, Yellow, Red 73

    Basic Spiritual Arcs of
- Green — Growth 81
- Blue — Training of the Ego 83
- Yellow — Illumination 85
- Red — Metamorphosis 87
- Purple — Spiritual Balance 91

Balancing Force of the Purple Arc 93

Analysis of the Relationships of the Basic Spiritual Rays 100

4. PUTTING COLOR TO WORK 105

Using the Inner Channel 108

How to Experience an Auric Viewing 110

How to Construct a Color Plume 117

How to Use a Color Prayer Plume or Visual Affirmation 118

Quick Color Remedies for Yourself or Others 119

The Lord's Prayer 121

The Lord's Prayer in Color 121

Mary Weddell's Meditation on the Lord's Prayer 123

Dr. George Weddell on Prayer 125

5. MARY'S INSIGHTS ON COLOR 127

6. EXCERPTS FROM PERTINENT WRITINGS 147

Glossary 169

Guide to Color Descriptions of the Rays 171

Guide to Meanings of the Color Rays 175

LIST OF ILLUSTRATIONS

Plate
    1. The Inner Channel 29
    2. Twelve Psychological Colors — Green 32
    3. Twelve Psychological Colors — Blue 33
    4. Twelve Psychological Colors — Yellow 36
    5. Twelve Psychological Colors — Red 37
    6. Two Color Prayers 40
    7. The Lord's Prayer in Color 41
    8. Twelve Basic Auric Rays — The Arc of Purple 44
    9. Twelve Basic Auric Rays — The Arc of Green 46
  10. Twelve Basic Auric Rays — The Arc of Blue 50
  11. Twelve Basic Auric Rays — The Arc of Yellow 54
  12. Twelve Basic Auric Rays — The Arc of Red 58

Diagram
    1. The Relationship of The Inner Channel to Man's Aura 21
    2. Diagram of a Color Plume — Available for Copying 111

PUBLISHER'S PREFACE

Three people merged their talents to receive and share the color knowledge that this book documents. Dr. George and Mary Weddell, students of ancient wisdom, were both clairvoyant, and they saw colors. They experimented for many years with these colors while seeking and testing the relationship of their meanings to those colors they saw inside and outside the human body. Miriam B. Willis, who was clairaudient, received additional material as she worked to bring the colors Mary saw into form to illustrate them. Then began, under Mary's guidance, Miriam's work of teaching this knowledge.

Each was prepared for his unique contribution by early life experiences and training. Each was sustained by a great faith that he was commissioned to bring this truth to mankind in the most accurate form possible. Each of their lives provided opportunities to prove the effectiveness of Creative Color.

Because their work has been beneficial and of great value to thousands, in America and abroad, we feel it should be available to all persons interested in the subject of color. Factual information and first hand experiences of teachers and students form the basis for this shared knowledge.

The Essene Fellowship of Peace approaches exoteric and esoteric Christianity in a flexible and non-denominational manner. It welcomes all seekers of truth. Fellowship members attempt to live and share the wisdom of early Essene teachings. The Fellowship believes that Jesus was raised by Essene parents in an Essene community and that many of their principles of living are applicable to life today.

Much material in this book is taken from the extended knowledge of ancient languages, esoteric truths and inspired guidance of Mary Weddell, mentor and master teacher. Knowledge of long lost color meanings, revealed to Mary, and development in the skills of using color she believed to be harmonious with what Jesus taught the disciples when he took them apart and taught them many things.

This book was prepared under the guidance of high spiritual beings by Miriam Willis and her committee of Fellowship members who are also ordained ministers and certified teachers of the color material. Our deep thanks go to all who have cooperated in the compilation and preparation of material for publication.

We welcome all readers seeking this knowledge and willingly share the color wisdom that we have, because we have benefitted from its use. It is hoped that this book can assist others in pursuing and extending knowledge of color and its usefulness to mankind.

—The Essene Fellowship of Peace

ACKNOWLEDGMENTS

As a teacher who has been given much credit throughout this book, I wish to thank those who have been given none. The highest compliment a teacher can receive is for a student to demonstrate the positive value of a teaching by applying it to his own life — and then to share the teaching with others. Mary Weddell and I have been fortunate in having many such students.

I thank all those who have contributed in any way to this book — students, printing advisors, readers. The Biographical Background chapter was written by Mary Weddell's granddaughter, a member of the Fellowship, and it has the approval of Mary's daughter, also a Fellowship member. It has been a challenging work requiring the great cooperation of many.

I wish especially to give credit to the three graduate teachers without whose commitment, perseverance, and selfless giving of their many talents over a period of years this book would never have been accomplished. They studied with Mary — and with me — for over twenty years and completed all the courses. It is no small task to reduce highly individualized, oral teaching to the printed page in language and style suitable to a general readership. This they have done through countless hours of compiling, writing, listening, editing, typing, etc. They are:

Margaret B. Branchflower,

Esther S. Barnes and

Miriam T. Abplanalp.

Miriam B. Willis, Senior Advisor

The Essene Fellowship of Peace

Hemet, California, February 20, 1988

INTRODUCTION

This book, "Creative Color" seeks to accomplish two things. First, to provide biographical background on the three people responsible for the knowledge of color it contains — a priceless legacy to humanity. And, second, to release to a wider field the results these pioneers achieved in their lifelong study and use of color.

This volume includes information on the history and development of the color material and the essential philosophy interweaving its use as well as a discussion of what color is. Special emphasis is given color as it envelops man in his aura. The detailed samples and definitions of over one hundred colors were all brought through from the higher planes. They form the basis for the special uses of color in self therapy, which aids spiritual growth. Illustrations, expanded meanings, suggestions regarding color prayer, selected inspirational writings and a detailed index of the colors complete the work.

Creative Color in its earlier years was taught individually and in classes. Teachers shared knowledge orally and in limited printed form. Students learned to prepare handmade samples of the colors. Now, due to advanced technology, accurate color samples, usable by the reader, are provided in this volume.

The basic material in this book can provide guidance for seekers after spiritual truths, and readers may develop considerable skill in the use of these color rays.

The philosophy of life underlying this book has a spiritual source. The great Christ principle of Love permeates it. It has no sectarian beliefs. It expresses a universal concept of life from which flows its basic premise: man is more than he appears to be, and through the creative power of color he can change himself for the better.

Through studying Creative Color as presented in this book man can see himself more clearly. Then, through conscious use of it he can make any necessary changes. Growth follows discovery, the little ego is awakened to the influence of the higher Self. Then man sees relationships and life experiences in a different light, the light of understanding. This empowers and catalyzes change. The result is spiritual balance, a pearl of great price, which becomes the keynote of his life.

MARY'S CHALLENGE AND PHILOSOPHY

A sympathetic reaction to color indicates capacity or readiness to accept and absorb the harmonious rays of color. The ideas presented to the seeker are as a spur to his development. The truth needed by each individual must come as a pure certainty from the depth of self, and not just as something which denies or affirms what has gone before. Only what is really needed by the individual, at the level of his understanding, can be recognized and properly valued. To this extent Truth is self-evident.

Color training represents an intuitive release of creative power through the color channel of one's being. Those who have come to respect intuition will find happy response to much that is presented in this color teaching. Those to whom intuition is a stranger will profit by working with color, for within the color teaching may be found the light so essential to a quickening within of the spiritual forces. And, from within the soul will come the approval. Color as a channel in our lives is a means of development over a God-given path of intelligent safety.

The seeker realizes that the harmonic response to the philosophy of the individual life might well be named "The Color Scheme", as color gives expression to that which lends warmth, beauty and illumination to life's path, easing the otherwise hard traveling, transforming the iron chain of obligation into the sparkling bejewelled golden thread of privilege.

A true seeker is ever about the business of living harmoniously with new measures of eternal values, thus enhancing that portion of the endless days of spirituality which are spent on earth. Man is only intelligent where he is able to get true or real results, only where he achieves.

* * *

After Mary Weddell's transition she gave the following message through Miriam Willis to graduating Color teachers. It is applicable to all who read this book.

Beloved ones, I would speak to you all from the depths of my heart. I would remind you that the power and strength that you build in the Christ center of your being comes to you through the faithful climbing of the beautiful colorful channel of your being, that lighted path that is the way, the truth and the life. And, you will say to me or others will say to you, 'And what is it that you say is colorful? Why do you not just call the path the lighted path? Is that not sufficient?' Beloved ones, it is truly all-sufficient, but the great Christ in this world is the light of the world. And His great emanation of light here o'ershadows, in truth, in infinite love, your earth. But, the Christ light is a purity beyond all conception, and you must grow the Christ within you to touch it. In the greatness of His love to you, He knows that He cannot send the whole of His being, and He provides you with the color rays which are resplendent in this heaven world.

Dear ones, these color rays hold within them the healing powers, the virtuous traits that overcame the world. Many of you are privileged to have been trained as healers in this pathway of color light and the gracious rays of the higher vibrations of the colors you have learned, yes, hundreds of them. You must in your life refresh your being with the knowledge of the quality of healing in these colors, for the world is sick and needs much healing . . . and more healers. How dare you know the right colors to use if you do not lift your whole being into the Christ Channel to the higher dimensions and listen, ever listen, to the guidance of His spirit to help you to know the harmonic flow of colors needed for the specific cause and intent of your prayer?

Be faithful, dear ones, be faithful in joy and the beauty of color, in the graciousness of its enfoldment about you. And, use the climbing meditative journey upward of your Channel morning and evening to strengthen the soul power of your being, the Christ center that can blossom in you. This is my heart's desire for you, because I know that color is a pathway for the saving of the world, even though there are thousands of people who do not know it. There will be a great burst of light through the scientists as well as through the religionists and the spiritual beings of the earth to bring this into blossoming.

Are you pioneers, among the first to spread the good news of this marvelous gift to change the world? He is, indeed, through you, each one contributing to the whole, the great Creator of all that you see of beauty and of usefulness about you. And, so He brings unto you a great blessing of peace and the joy and the developing power in color rays that you know so well to use.

My love overshadows you, my very dear ones, like my own children. God bless you.

* * *

The following article, discovered among Mary's writings after her transition, reveals an important part of the philosophy undergirding her teaching on Color.

The entire world is a musical instrument. I believe, earthly music is an echo of the Cosmic harmony; it is a relic of heaven.

The processes of creation or construction are all dependent upon the vibrational power of tone. The Universe is builded to music.

The numerical power of twelve is the highest spiritual emanation active in the Universe, whereas seven transforms that power into the concreting and building forces that operate on the physical plane.

The twelve semitones of the chromatic scale and the seven notes of the diatonic are numeral divisions corresponding to the cosmic pattern of our solar system.

Spiritual science teaches that the path of human progression in our present evolutionary scheme extends through seven aeonic days and five cosmic nights. It is in keeping with this evolutionary pattern that the spectrum shows seven colors which are seen with ordinary sight "as clear as day," but with five more colors discernable only to etheric vision, or the sight that sees even in the dark of night. On the musical keyboard these days and nights are also in evidence as seven white keys and five black.

Major tones create objectively and minor tones build subjectively. As man works consciously in the outer world under the impulses of major notes, so also does he work subjectively on the inner planes in developing and expanding his faculties under the influence of minor tones.

The major notes (keys) are outpouring, productive, expanding. The minor notes (keys) are secretive, sustaining, enfolding.

The keyboard of the piano is composed of eighty-eight keys, which number reduces numerologically to seven.

Every sound emanates a certain color and takes on a definite form. Conversely, every form gives forth a sound; that sound is its key note.

On the back of the first page of this manuscript Mary had written a line of characters she identified as Sanskrit. Her translation of this was:

> Knowledge itself is there; bereft of covering and impurities,
> becoming infinite, the knowable becomes small.

— Mary D. Weddell

Chapter 1

BIOGRAPHICAL BACKGROUND

*Three life streams of consciousness brought
this river of color knowledge to the world.*

As the storm clouds of World War I began to dominate the landscape of Europe, a tiny American woman sat at the side of a hospital bed in Seattle, Washington, quietly watching the flow of colors around a gravely ill patient and observing changes of the gray area in the patient's aura into healthy and colorful light. This little woman was Mary Dies Weddell. The place was a private hospital owned and operated by her husband, Dr. George Weddell. Mary often went to the hospital to give comfort and to channel healing colors to the many diseased patients.

Before wholistic medicine was even a seed in the mind of today's medical community, Dr. George and Mary treated the whole person, guided by attunement with God Power. These two individuals possessed a rare affinity beyond that of a conventional, happily married couple, an affinity of mind and spirit which made their collaboration far more than the sum of its parts.

Little did Mary know while she sat by the bedside of those patients, that in Toronto, Canada, a young girl entering an Episcopal convent would some day become her pupil, companion and teacher of her work.

The story of this unusual trio begins with the birth of George Washington Weddell in 1881, on a farm near Ashland, Ohio. A middle child in a family of eight, George was a sunny boy with red-gold curls, big blue eyes, an infectious grin, precocious beyond his years. By the age of ten he was interested in chemistry and he attended lectures open to the public but usually attended by adults. At eighteen he was teaching in a country school near the farm and riding his horse to Ashland to take trigonometry and other classes preparatory to entering college. It took two years of teaching to save the money to study to be an osteopathic physician.

One summer during his school vacation, George and another student accompanied a patient to Germany to care for him and see him settled. In return they were to receive roundtrip tickets and room and board along the way. When they got to Germany, the man disappeared leaving them with no money nor tickets. While earning their passage back, George and his friend attended a lecture by a famous German doctor who practiced what was called "bloodless surgery". He was demonstrating a case of hip dislocation. The common practice at that time for a dislocation of that kind was surgery. The doctor looked into the circle of students around him and pointed to George saying, "You with the blue eyes, come and assist me." George stayed longer than he had planned and learned many innovative techniques about manipulation of bones and joints. Throughout his career, George was always open to new ideas and methods. After completing the osteopathic course, George took a job teaching anatomy at Drake University to pay his way while studying for a medical degree. He became an accredited physician and surgeon, both a Doctor of Osteopathy and a Medical Doctor. It was during those years that he met and married Mary.

One of George's many talents was a beautiful tenor voice and a life-long love of music. In 1904, he and an older brother joined a chorus assembled for the Welsh festival Eisteddfod. His brother became interested in a vivacious blonde soprano. As it happened, her older sister, Mary, was singing contralto and the four became close friends.

Mary was George's opposite: tiny where he was robust, with thick, dark auburn hair, sparkling brown eyes, a quiet, self-effacing manner and a tendency to take life just a bit too seriously. George had the demeanor of a troubador, laughing, singing, telling jokes and playing pranks. Mary adored him on sight but never fully comprehended what he saw in such a shy little brown wren, as she thought herself to be. This tendency not to see her own uniqueness and excellence and to be embarrassed by attention and adulation was to follow her throughout her life.

She entered the world as Mary Elizabeth Dies in 1886 in Santa Ana, California, but she and her five siblings were raised in Des Moines, Iowa. Her father was a skilled cabinet maker and house builder. He traveled throughout Iowa, building groups of houses, a forerunner of our modern housing tracts. Mary's mother, the consummate matriarch, raised six foster children as well as her own six and helped to raise several of Mary's generation as well. This family provided fertile ground for Mary's innate psychic abilities, as both of her parents were "sensitives" in their own right. Home remedies and motherly care of the sick took on an added dimension when Mary's mother was in charge. It was a boisterous, energetic, intellectual and creative family where Mary, like her quiet, dreaming father, was often to be found in the background. Mary saw lights around people and was very sensitive to changes of mood and feeling in others. Her talents were never discouraged but neither were they given an explanation or frame of reference.

Mary's classical education included Latin and Greek. In addition, her study of opera taught her to sing and read French and Italian. All of these languages were to be of assistance in later years as she became a serious biblical scholar. After high school, Mary entered a music conservatory in Des Moines to study piano for a music certificate. The culmination of this effort was to take place several years later, when in possession of the certificate, she was chosen to perform for the Boston Conservatory of Music.

It was a year after their first meeting that George was able to persuade Mary that he was as enamored of her as she was of him. They were married when she was nineteen and he twenty-four, temporarily moving in with her parents. This beginning was to be the dominant pattern of their lives; multi-generational living, houses filled with people of a variety of relationships. Dr. George's only known regret in this union was a periodic yearning to have his Mary to himself. A year after their marriage, Mary gave birth to their only child, Constance, in 1906. To Mary's sorrow and deep regret, she was never able to have more children. Mary's strong maternal instincts, combined with spiritual power, were, however, to make her a mother figure to dozens of people throughout her life.

By early 1912, Dr. George and Mary each had a brother living in Seattle, Washington urging them to move west. Later that year they did so and it didn't take long for both sets of parents to follow suit. Dr. George took over part of a medical practice from a doctor who was in failing health at the time. They moved in with the doctor's family and were hardly settled in their new life when Mary suddenly awoke one morning unable to walk. Her legs were completely paralyzed. Many doctors, including the Mayo brothers who were in Seattle attending a convention, examined her. It was never finally determined what the cause was, but it was suspected that infected tonsils poisoned her system. The doctors had no cure and little hope for her recovery.

Dr. George and Mary, however, never lost faith in her ultimate release from this prison. To understand her agony it is necessary to examine how she had been used to spending her time: caring for Constance, running a large household, making her own and her child's clothes, moving frequently, usually redecorating and making curtains, plus entertaining elegantly and paying for a portion of the family expenses by teaching piano. All of a sudden she couldn't walk, couldn't sit at her beloved piano and life went on around her but without her. To pass the time and keep up her spirits, a missionary friend who had recently returned from the Middle East, taught her Sanskrit and from that root she studied Aramaic and Ancient Hebrew. This afforded her an opportunity to read the Bible in the King James version, in Latin, in Greek, in Aramaic and in Ancient Hebrew, and to read the ancient writings that pre-date but relate to the text. This perspective through time was to give her a view of Christianity both scholarly and basic, the ability to see that which changes with time and that which remains constant. Her study of the Essenes of Jesus' time was to influence a great deal her approach to religious expression.

Mary bore her affliction for nearly a year, but some months into this period something strange happened. One night the nurse found Mary standing by the window looking out. Wisely, she didn't awaken Mary but observed her returning to the bed. After this incident, Mary began to dream over and over that she was walking but continued to walk only in her sleep.

Concurrently with this walking pattern, she began to see white light and then color swirling around her, the first time in a rainbow pattern and then shifting, ever changing patterns of light surrounding her. She began to perceive that when this happened she felt better. She asked in prayer for the meaning of this phenomenon and through automatic writing was gradually given the meanings of the colors. Over time, through her acceptance of the healing color rays and the sleep-walking, feeling began to return to her legs and she was able to stand, then to walk first a few steps, and then gradually at a normal pace. Given the richness of learning and experiencing during that year of confinement, one cannot help but wonder if it was not a necessary respite in her busy life to allow her to obtain the tools with which to meet her destiny.

After Mary' recovery, Dr. George leased a large building in Seattle and equipped it as a convalescent hospital. This was the beginning of their collaboration in health care and in experimentation with the use of color. Mary sometimes would view the patient and note areas of the aura which were gray or discolored in relation to the surrounding colors. She would mentally send specific colors to the patient's aura depending on the diagnosis of what was needed. Often she was not in the presence of the patient at all but clairvoyantly saw him and so pinpointed the area of difficulty.

Independent from her information, Dr. George made his own diagnosis on medical grounds. Even that early in his career he was highly regarded as a diagnostician. He added a rare kind of psychic ability of his own. He could literally see through the human body so that if there were a misshapen organ, an extra growth, discolored or blocked organs or blood vessels, he was able to see with the inner eye as well as to diagnose from symptoms. He was active as a surgeon and throughout his life had a remarkable record for patient survival during and after surgery. One reason was that his ability to see into the body also enabled him to tell whether or not a patient could withstand the stress of surgery at any specific point in time. On all of his surgical patients, he and Mary would deduce separately when the time was propitious and then together set the date and time, using color healing in the interim to better prepare the patient for the trauma of surgery.

These early years, beginning in Seattle, were the testing ground for color as a therapeutic technique, and Mary was able to be involved directly with the work. Their daughter Constance was interested in art from an early age and Mary, who had no artistic abilities, used the watercolors available at home to show Dr. George the colors she was seeing and using as they discussed a particular case. Mary saw the colors leaving her in the form of a feather. Thus, she used the word "plume" for combinations of colors arranged like blocks, one upon the other, in specific sequences. This term and that configuration of colors is still used by her students today. Before her teaching days these plumes were of a temporary nature as she could carry all the visual and verbal images in her mind, and color was a constant, ever changing part of her visual universe. There have been others who could see and read auras, few, however, have had the ability to read the physical, mental-emotional and spiritual fields simultaneously as Mary did. She was able to differentiate between colors which were pertinent to the psychology of the individual in contrast to those that would affect the spiritual side of the nature, as well as see the holes, gray areas or out of balance indications that signalled physical disease.

Early in her work she formed a method of working which was either charming or frustrating to the recipient, depending upon his own psychological stance. She was a great story teller and known as the "story-telling lady" at Children's Hospital, where the children adored her. To adults, she would tell a story, usually homespun, sometimes humorous, and frequently unrelated to the listener in any discernible way. At the same time she would read the aura, note imbalances and channel energy and color to the needy condition of the listener. People were drawn to her and remarked how much better they felt after seeing her, but few had any idea of what she was actually doing.

In 1916 Dr. George, Mary and her parents purchased and operated a sanatorium at Soap Lake, Washington. This facility was close to the banks of the lake. The patients came primarily for the mineral baths. They would be immersed in the mud up to their necks and be given mineral water from the natural springs to drink. There are still sanatoriums of this type in the area. Dr. George and Mary continued their study and use of color throughout this period of their lives.

Mary's focus primarily on the spiritual rather than on physical health in the teaching of color reflected her own spiritual evolution. Although she was brought up in the Episcopal Church, her natural philosophical and spiritual leanings, as well as those of her parents, encouraged a wide exploration of reading matter. Before leaving Des Moines, the family was well versed in Theosophy and studied and contributed to the "Great Work" series of books. Upon moving to Seattle, they broadened this knowledge and joined a group simply called "The Brotherhood". This connection was to follow Mary throughout the balance of her life even though the group was spiritually directed to disperse worldwide some years later. This preparation and her subsequent study of religious works written in ancient languages, was to give her a universal perspective on what "Christ Consciousness" truly is.

While Mary and Dr. George were continuing their work with color, Miriam Barr Willis was beginning her period of service as an Episcopal Sister in Canada. This remarkable lady began her life in 1895 in London, Ontario, as the youngest in a family of seven children. Her artistic abilities evidenced early and were expressed through drawing and playing the piano. The family lived a proper, genteel city life until Miriam was ten when her father decided to move the family to Alberta in order to take advantage of free land under the homestead provisions of the day. Much optimistic government advertising had assured the adventurous easterners that snow in the west was nearly non-existent and the overall weather picture ideal. Six months before the ladies of the family left Ontario, Miriam's father and brothers went out west to build a new home. They erected a large, two story house, expecting to duplicate the amenities of their usual life style. In fact, the transportation of furniture, household goods, even including a modern furnace, took two railway cars. The ranch was seventy miles from the nearest railroad and when all these possessions arrived they were transferred to wagons to finish the trip. As a portent of events to come, the rest of the family arrived in November and had to wait until a blizzard passed to begin the last leg of the journey.

The next seven years were often harsh, with drought, blizzards and prairie fires a frequent threat. However, being a happy family of adventurous personalities, the freedom and fun of outdoor life held great appeal.

Miriam rode horseback frequently and fell occasionally. One of these falls at age fifteen resulted in a serious injury to the spine causing paralysis. For a time she couldn't move sufficiently to take the arduous journey to seek medical care. When the paralysis partially passed, her brother made her a set of crutches, and it was lucky he did. Before the family had a chance to get help for Miriam, a prairie fire was upon them. It was heading straight for the house when Miriam hobbled out to a plowed field with her mother who carried as many of the household goods as she was able. Her father and brothers were desperately fighting the fire while Miriam and her mother sat in the field and prayed. At the last moment the wind shifted and spared the house. Some livestock were lost. Much of the surrounding land was made useless for grazing. When the crisis passed, Miriam was sent to the hospital, a trip consisting of seventy miles by wagon and eighteen hours on the train.

One of her early psychic experiences occurred at this time. She was lying on her back at night and could see a star outside the window of her hospital room. The star spoke to her and said she would recover and devote her life to missionary work. Miriam felt this to be true. The idea was not foreign to her as the family were devout Episcopalians and prayed together daily. Miriam received treatment all summer in the hospital; then in the autumn she convalesced at her eldest sister's home. By the time she was ready to return home, the paralysis was gone and she walked without assistance. However, her spine was twisted in such a way that her lower back has been a lifelong problem for her.

When it was time to return home, there was no money to pay her fare. Miriam's family decided to sell one of the cows which had never been a cooperative giver of milk. Mrs. Willis was very worried that the cow would act in her usual manner when the buyer came to look her over. She stood at the window and prayed while the transaction, including a milking demonstration, was progressing. To everyone's amazement the cow never so much as switched her tail from start to finish. The family was paid the exact amount of Miriam's fare home. Miriam's trip home was uneventful until her trunk would not fit into the wagon and had to be left temporarily in town. Miriam had promised her sister not to tell that the trunk was loaded with fresh fruit as a surprise for the family. By the time the trunk was recovered, the fruit had frozen, then melted and ruined all of her clothes. But Miriam, as always, had kept her word that the gift would be a surprise.

Shortly after her return, Miriam's father took a job in Castor, Alberta, as manager of several lumber yards. The family left the ranch and never returned. They moved again to Calgary, but then Miriam left them, going to Toronto as nurse to her pregnant sister-in-law. Three of Miriam's brothers were in Toronto also, two of them at Trinity College. There Miriam met Jack, the man she was to love all of her life. This love was not to come to fruition for World War I interfered. Jack joined the army and was sent to England and subsequently to France. Miriam learned later, from her brother George, that Jack had a premonition of his own death and for this reason had not declared his love. He was killed in action not long after arriving in France.

It is at this point in the story that the invisible threads that interwove the lives of Dr. George, Mary and Miriam began their tapestry. One of Miriam's brothers was sent to New York on scholarship to the Theological Seminary and took a job as assistant to the rector of St. Anne's Church in the Bronx. The Rector was to later become the Episcopal Bishop of Los Angeles and his wife's sister, Edith, the link by which the three principals of the story were finally joined. Miriam's brother was strongly attracted to Edith and she to him. Because of their friendship, Miriam was invited to visit Edith's family in New Canaan, Connecticut, and the two girls became and remained close friends.

Because of the war, Miriam's family dispersed to several widely separate locations and she was working as a governess in Toronto. It was at this time that she met the administrator of the hospital run by the Sisters of St. John the Divine. She became interested in enrolling in the nursing school. However, the more she talked to the Sisters, the more she began to see herself as a part of the religious community as well. After serious thought, she decided to join the Order and train as a nursing sister. Soon after she joined the Order, Jack came to her in a vision while she was in the chapel. He knelt beside her, put his hand over hers and she knew immediately that he was dead. The Reverend Mother called her shortly afterward to give her a telegram, but she already knew what it said.

The next few years were spent in the operating room where Miriam became an expert surgical nurse. She also taught other nurses operating room skills, the first in a long line of teaching assignments. Nursing and teaching skills have been repeatedly needed all of her life.

The end of Miriam's formal nursing career came when a serious attack of jaundice, caused by a chronically weak liver strained by overwork, convinced those in authority that a less strenuous career was in order. She was sent to the University to study teaching. Finishing fourth in her class, she was denied a certificate due to the fact that she did not have a high school diploma. The lack of certificate did not hamper her career as long as she was a Sister, but later, when she left the convent, it prevented her from teaching on the outside.

After her teaching course, she was assigned to a girls' boarding school where she taught elementary age children. Combining art with geography and history delighted the children and made them more willing to deal with the other basics. Her favorite teaching assignment was a seven year stint at St. Christina's in Cooperstown, New York, where she introduced art, music and physical education to the school. With her characteristic ingenuity, she made contact with members of the New York Actors' Guild through the Little Church Around the Corner in New York City. She persuaded those talented people to accept part time employment at the school for room and board only, teaching art, music and drama to the children there as well as at the summer camp. Miriam traveled extensively with the Mother Superior, holding retreats for women and recruiting novices for the Order. Eventually she was made Assistant Superior of the Order.

One of her tasks was to be in charge of the infirmary, the closest she would be to her old nursing days. Miriam, like Mary and Dr. George, had a talent for combining physical with spiritual healing. One incident during infirmary days illustrates the point. One of the younger Sisters, a beautiful and musical girl, had persistent ulcers in her mouth. She had been treated repeatedly but nothing seemed to help. One day she confided to Miriam that her childhood had been a tragic time and expressed her inability to let it go. They sat together on Miriam's sofa and prayed. Miriam advised the Sister to write down every one of the painful memories then and there. Miriam prayed silently as the girl wrote sixteen pages. Then Miriam took her to the fireplace and suggested she burn the pages and to KNOW while they were burning that every one of those memories was vanishing forever from her life. The next morning the young Sister came rushing in grinning happily. Miriam told her to open her mouth so she could treat the ulcers. The girl just kept grinning. Finally, she opened her mouth and Miriam saw that all of the ulcers were gone.

Miriam's spiritual "sight" began early in life but was sporadic. One example from her teens took place on a train ride to Castor. She had a precognitive experience of teaching a spiritual message to a large audience. The lecture went through her mind and was far beyond her knowledge and comprehension of spirituality at that time in her life. She has since given that talk and similar ones many times.

During the last years in the convent, when she was functioning as Assistant Superior, Miriam began a healing group. This was a controversial step as the more conservative sisters thought prayer and communion were the only proper forms of devotion. However, she persevered. The Mother Superior and the Bishop both supported her work. This was gratifying to her as both of these individuals had been instrumental in bringing her into the religious life and she had great respect for them. The Bishop at one point expressed his intent to give a series of lectures at the convent on the theme of healing. He died before this could take place, but Miriam continued to see him in spirit and his support of her subsequent actions was important to her conviction that her decisions were in tune with God's plan for her. Miriam saw many people on the "other side" during her development as a Sister, and this mystical side of her nature has continued to grow and develop.

Miriam remained a part of the Sisterhood for twenty-five years. During the months just prior to leaving she was increasingly troubled about her commitment to the Order. She had talked to the Chaplain and attempted to consult with her Mother Superior but was unsuccessful. Shortly before the final decision was made, Miriam was awakened one night by a large figure of a man who at the time she thought was Jesus, who stood in front of her bed, pointed at her and said, "GO YE!" in a commanding voice. He was carrying a small evergreen tree which he threw out the window facing her bed. She saw the roofs of many houses appear, each with an evergreen on its roof. The trees burst into flame. She KNEW it was a spiritual fire. The man kept repeating "GO YE!" During this visitation Miriam reacted to the command of "GO YE!" with lamentations about all of her responsibilities. The Visitor stared at her and repeated "GO YE!" Miriam had in fact five areas of convent responsibility, but soon after the spiritual visitation they were one by one given to others through no effort on her part. When tasks were removed, her superior attempted to give her a ceramic art studio, but by this time she was paying attention to her feelings and inner guidance and asked that this not be done.

Unbeknownst to Miriam, during these months of turmoil, Mary, who now lived in Los Angeles, knew Miriam was to be her student and was clairvoyantly "seeing" the convent and the individual Sisters at their tasks as well as knowing what was happening in Miriam's mind and heart. In her own quiet way Mary was nudging Miriam to action. Mary knew no names at this time, just pictures of faces and scenes in her head.

Miriam's opportunity to leave the convent came about through Edith, Miriam's old friend from New York. Although now married, with teenage children, and living in the Los Angeles area, Edith kept in touch with both Miriam and her brother. It was part of the system of the Order that one did not communicate to outsiders the kinds of doubts and emotional turmoil that Miriam was experiencing. However, she was allowed to write to her brother and he, in turn, told Edith. By chance, or was it chance, Edith and her family were in Detroit to purchase a new car shortly after Miriam was left with no duties and the conviction she must leave. Her problem was no money and no way to earn a living. Edith's husband, after picking up their car in Detroit, wanted to visit a friend who had been badly burned as a result of an accident and was convalescing in a Toronto hospital.

While he was at the hospital Edith called Miriam and paid her a visit; it was Labor Day, 1941. To her embarrassed astonishment Edith kept hearing a voice saying over and over, "Take her back to California with you." She tried to keep her attention on their conversation, but the voice kept distracting her. Finally, in a quiet tone and sheepish manner, she asked, "Do you think you could come back to California with me?" Miriam promptly surprised herself by saying, "Yes, I could. I am due for my rest time right about now." Miriam then asked the Acting Superior if she could go to California, wondering, also, if it would be possible to get permission from the Ministry of the Interior in Ottawa. This formality was a recent requirement due to World War II. Several American Sisters had been waiting for some time with no word on when they would be able to return home for their rest time.

The Acting Superior sent a telegram to the Minister of the Interior, whom she knew. He replied almost immediately, saying, "I will see her at 9:00 A.M. Tuesday morning. Tell her to take the four o'clock train." The Sisters gave Miriam money; she went to Ottawa and found her way around the strange city as if it were her home town. She was amazed at how familiar it seemed. The night before her appointment she could hardly sleep. She felt herself surrounded with heavenly beings. The Bishop was among them urging her on, and she thought, "This is of God because if it were not of God the man who ordained me would not be urging me to leave." The next morning she went to the Immigration Office and met the man who was to approve her papers. He asked how long she wanted to be away, and she said, "Three months. I may have a commission to paint a portrait there, and I will need time to earn my fare back." A small smile tugged at his lips as he stamped her papers and handed them back. He looked at her directly and said, "The visa is good for a year, and the passport for ten years." She exclaimed with surprise. He merely smiled. Mary was to tell her later that all of these coincidental and fortunate events were foreordained and that the Minister and the Immigration Agent were part of the "Brotherhood" of which Mary and Dr. George had been a part since their early days in Seattle. It gave Miriam confidence to hear that, for it confirmed her inner guidance.

During the decades of Miriam's sojourn with the Sisters, Mary and Dr. George continued their medical and spiritual work, their knowledge shared only with Mary's parents. They lived in a succession of homes in Washington and California. Their daughter Constance attended fourteens schools before high school graduation. In 1923, the family made their first trip to California, Dr. George being the catalyst for this venture. He and a pharmacist friend had developed a skin cancer salve and Dr. George had contracted with a large California city to test it on prisoners in the city jails. Concurrently with this project, Dr. George enrolled in a six month diagnostic course with an osteopath in Riverside, California, who had invented a machine with techniques similar to modern ultrasonics.

The trip from Seattle to Los Angeles was in keeping with their usual life style. The caravan consisted of three cars containing seven adults, five children and the family dog and cat. As if this were not complex enough, they camped out at night. In those days city parks provided travelers with public camping spaces and comfort facilities. Now this was not a family who had ever dealt with "roughing it", so camping consisted of setting up tents, beds, cook stoves and tables each and every night for three weeks. After years in cool, rainy Washington they arrived in Los Angeles in early October to be greeted by a temperature of a hundred and four degrees. They found a camping spot in Elysian Park, which is just north of the present Dodger Stadium. Fortunately, they soon found a suitable house in Eagle Rock near Occidental College as their first home.

Dr. George commuted between Riverside and Los Angeles for six months while completing his classes and overseeing the testing of his cancer salve. This salve destroyed certain kinds of skin cancer cells and prevented the necessity of surgical removal. When the experiment was complete and successful, Dr. George donated the formula for the use of humanity. He had been a charter member of the White Cross, a cancer society, and continued in cancer research. He later created a second, post surgical salve to be used where large indentations had occurred after cancers were removed. The salve brought the skin together and healed it without scarring. The following year the family was recalled to Washington where Dr. George had accepted a position with the Immigration Service. The location was Blaine, and, in addition to working for the United States Government Dr. George maintained a private practice in his home.

Vancouver was not far away on the Canadian side of the border, and the family went often to visit a professor and his wife whom they had met during one of their residences in Seattle. This family was a member of the Oxford Group, which was begun in England by Dr.

Frank Buchman and later referred to as Moral Rearmament.[1] Edith, Miriam's friend, had become involved with the group in California and in 1924 was attending one of their meetings in Vancouver at the same time Dr. George and Mary were visiting their professor friend. Edith was immediately attracted to the tiny woman named Mary who played the piano with the sureness and command of a large man. She was further intrigued later in the evening to find that this same little lady sang in a resonant contralto voice, had a four-octave range, and displayed the same virtuosity as her instrumental style. One of the premises of the Oxford Group was that everyone had problems, and it was the task of the members to find those areas in the new arrival and offer assistance. Edith was assigned to Mary, but to her puzzlement, could find nothing wrong with her. Gradually she became aware that Mary was counseling her rather than the other way around. This meeting was the beginning of a friendship and teacher-pupil relationship which lasted until Edith's death in 1960.

The household in Blaine was a typical example of the family life style. It was a large, two-story, frame house overlooking the bay. Besides the three generations in the immediate family, two nieces and a nephew had become permanent members of the household. In addition, a former patient had moved in and several of either Dr. George's or Mary's nieces and nephews, at any given time, were dropped off for weeks or months depending on their parents' desires. The family nickname for this establishment was "The Weddell Hotel". The children, especially the younger ones, were hard pressed to explain this menage to school friends. On any given day the one doing the explaining might not know everyone himself, especially at dinner. Twenty was a normal number, and the kitchen was always ready for more. Both sides of this family had an almost tribal consciousness; they seemed to have no difficulty moving from one group to another, the only criterion apparently being what seemed to make sense at any point in time.

In 1927 all headed back to California for the sake of Dr. George's health. He had had a series of bouts with flu and decided that a dry climate would stimulate an improvement in his health, which it did. The early 1930's were an important turning point for the family. In a three year period Constance and the nieces were all married from the family home and Mary's beloved father died.

In 1937 Dr. George and Mary purchased a house in Glendale which was to be the closest thing to a permanent home they ever had. It was an authentic Mediterranean style house which could have been moved to a canal in Venice, Italy, and no one would have blinked an eye. It was Dr. George's favorite home, and they were extremely happy there. To add to their joy that year, Constance presented them with their only grandchild.

It was during the 1930's and 1940's that Dr. George and Mary began to share their work. Much of what they believed, studied and worked with simply would not have been accepted in earlier years and in a more conservative locale. Their first class contained one hundred doctors and dentists, many with first hand knowledge of Dr. George's remarkable cure rate and a desire to improve their own. Later Mary began to give classes on Color once a week in Bel Air and Beverly Hills. She had students from England and France where she developed quite a following. Those countries showed a greater eagerness for New Thought

---

[1] The group philosophy and methods were based on Christian beliefs. The purpose was to bring people together to solve personal problems and thereby evolve a method for collectively solving those of nations.

than did most of the United States at that time. Mary and Dr. George were still very private people and most of the family were not privy to the beliefs and activities which were fundamental to their way of life.

Before Miriam left the convent Mary began to see clairvoyantly at least a dozen Sisters, their individual rooms, and the Chapel. The detail she related later to Miriam was astonishing. She could describe the carved wood and the bronze and gold angels with decorations of pearls. She saw Sisters walking and talking and could describe their size, shape, ways of moving and their personalities. Among the Sisters, she saw Miriam and knew her to be a highly spiritual individual to whom she would later act as teacher and mentor.

In late 1941, shortly after arriving in California, Miriam was invited by Edith to accompany her to a dinner party at a friend's home where Mary and Dr. George were also to be present. The house was a large Spanish style home with a long, sunken living room. Miriam entered the room wearing her nun's habit. From the far end of the room a small, elegantly clad lady with a big smile came across to her with hands outstretched and said, "You have come at last, oh, you've come at last." Miriam had no idea what Mary meant and thought she was merely being gracious. From that meeting began an intense and unique relationship which was to bring an expansion and fulfillment to the spiritual aspirations of both women. Not long after they met, Mary asked Miriam to live with her and to nurse her mother, who was failing rapidly. Miriam cared for Mary's mother through the last months of her life. In the process Miriam was adopted emotionally and spiritually by four generations of this family, and has remained to this day a priceless treasure to all of them.

By the time Miriam's one year visa was about to expire, she knew she would never go back to the convent and that Mary was the spiritual teacher she had been seeking. Miriam had spent six months before leaving the convent trying to obtain an interview with the ailing Mother Superior to tell her of her doubts and growing conviction that she would have to leave. When Miriam wrote that she was not returning they urged her to come back, but she reminded them of her attempts to seek counsel in the past and stated she knew her life had undergone an irrevocable change. In order to get permanent residence status, Miriam had to return to Canada and re-enter the United States as a registered alien. On leaving Canada the year before she had been allowed to take only twenty-five dollars out of the country. In the United States she was allowed only to receive gifts of money while on a visitor's visa. Thus, except for room, board and a few monetary gifts, she was essentially penniless. She arrived in Vancouver, British Columbia, with limited funds, expecting a short, orderly process of re-entry. Instead, the process dragged out to nine weeks during which time she ran out of funds and had to go to live with one of her sisters in a nearby city.

In addition to finding Miriam, two climactic events took place for Mary in the early 1940's. One was the death of Mary's mother with whom she had lived nearly all of her life. The second and most difficult was the sudden death of Dr. George. He was involved in an automobile accident where a child in the other car was hurt. He hurried to the rescue, doctor bag in hand, had a heart attack at the scene and was dead on arrival at the hospital. This was the most difficult period of Mary's life. She was, for a time, nearly immobilized by grief. She needed all of her faith and self-discipline to find direction and solace. Constance and her family decided to move in with Mary to assist her in dealing with the loss. Because of the war, Constance's husband was working two jobs, and Mary became housekeeper and babysitter while Constance helped keep her husband's business going. When Constance wasn't playing secretary, she was standing in line with food ration coupons and riding the bus to save gasoline rations. Somehow, in spite of war and rationing and deaths in the family, when they gathered together for dinner an abundance of people, food, laughter and love still prevailed.

Mary contracted pernicious anemia during this period and was not expected to live long. However, two doctor friends working in experimental medicine came to her weekly for many years, to give her injections of some kind. Miriam and Constance never saw them except at a distance, and the whole procedure was handled privately and quietly. The treatments gradually became further apart and, after the death of one of the doctors, ceased altogether. By that time Mary was nearly ninety and thirty-five years had elapsed. The treatments and Mary's spirit had prevailed.

While Mary was adjusting to her changing circumstances, Miriam was venturing out on her own. Shortly before Dr. George died she had obtained her first salaried job after returning to California. She had spent several days with little money, making long bus rides, trying to find work to no avail. Finally, at breakfast one morning, Dr. George handed her a business card and said the gentleman in question was in the pottery business and was looking for help. She suspected that Dr. George had had a hand in this but thanked him politely and tried to figure out how to get there. She was down to five cents and was too proud to tell Dr. George or Mary she did not have busfare. As she sat down to her daily devotions she found ten dollars in her Bible. The job was hers by the end of the day, and a decade of creative work in ceramics followed. The pottery company specialized in small animal figures. Whenever a particular function was shortstaffed, Miriam would fill in. In this way she became adept at painting, glazing, mold making and the use of the kiln. The final opportunity to hone her skills came when she went to work for a woman who designed ceramic flowers. Miriam was given a job as designer, and created many beautiful floral displays for tables and wall hangings.

In 1944, Miriam decided to go into the ceramics business for herself. She rented a hillside apartment in Pasadena which had two downstairs rooms perfect for her work and a large upstairs living area. At first sight this did not appear to be an auspicious location. The stairway was filled with stones and dirt, nearly impassable. Upstairs the glass was gone from the windows. Food, empty liquor bottles and general debris covered the entire floor. However, a voice kept saying, "This is the place," over and over, so Miriam, trusting this inner voice, agreed to sign a lease. It turned out that, like events before and others after, the Brotherhood, through the landlord, had had a hand in this choice.

Miriam had been settled for a short time when a gentleman appeared at her door and requested that she work for him designing and producing Chinese figurines. She stated that she was not interested as she wished to work for herself and, besides, her knowledge of glazing was sketchy. However, he was not to be deterred and stated that money was no object. She thought to herself that the man was crazy, but if he was willing to pay her to learn on his time, why not? She barely started producing the figures when it became apparent that he wanted a volume operation which was impossible from her two small rooms. Not to be daunted, she set out to find larger quarters only to discover that the war effort had made rental space nearly impossible to find. Finally, in South Pasadena she discovered a large upstairs room available and proceeded to set up a kiln and build benches and tables.

No sooner was the second firing of the first batch begun when a man appeared at the door and said that the Government needed the space, and she was evicted. There was nothing to do but to add onto the downstairs rooms at her studio. Finding wood for construction, not to mention skilled labor, was nearly impossible during the war. Fortunately, her employer had also contracted with the local fire department to make wooden trays in their spare time and Miriam was the quality control inspector. She prevailed upon the firemen to do construction work on their days off. They haunted junk yards until they found enough piano cases to build the walls and roof. The firemen installed the electricity which she insisted they inspect themselves. Although they were paid, it took liberal doses of pie, coffee, ice cream and wheedling to keep them on the time schedule needed. When the war ended the market for mass-produced figurines quickly collapsed as less expensive imports began to arrive. Miriam also created high quality specialty figurines, flowers and birds. She displayed her work annually at art trade shows, where she sold to better department stores in Los Angeles, New York City, Chicago and Seattle.

Miriam's old friend Edith had a twin sister, Violet, who lost her husband in 1948 and was lonely living in a large, two-story house on a half acre in South Pasadena. Violet asked Miriam to live with her. To assist her, Violet permitted Miriam to turn a building at the rear of the property into a ceramics studio. Miriam's work took a religious turn at this time, and she sold primarily through church sponsored art shows. She created a beautiful Madonna, which was very popular, a charming St. Francis and a unique creche set that most of her friends have seen and admired through the years. A few more birds and flowers and a fountain or two completed the repertoire. Miriam always combined the spiritual with the creative, and she needed to do so at this time. The plaster molds for some of her figures, when filled with liquid clay, weighed sixty pounds. When lifting and turning the molds she would fill herself with God power and was so filled with strength she would simply pick up a casting and turn it. Mary taught her to use Color to refine her techniques of lifting and moving. When they later lived together they would rearrange the furniture, together. It must have been a sight, seeing two small, not so young women carrying furniture around with cheerful confidence. To this day, in her nineties and weighing scarcely one hundred pounds, Miriam moves her bed the same way.

During the period after Dr. George's death in 1943, and for a number of years, Mary taught Color classes in other people's homes in the Los Angeles area. In 1954, Mary left her Glendale home to live with a friend. They rented a house owned by Violet which was across the garden from Miriam's studio. It was during the next decade that the intense work by Miriam and Mary took place to produce on paper what Mary saw in auras. Mary would describe the color and Miriam would work with oil crayons to duplicate it. Mary coached her through her mistakes until the color was right and would then give Miriam the meaning. Then they would go on to the next one. Eventually the fans, or arcs, shown in the Color Plates of this book were created by this collaboration. After the color fans were complete, which took over a year, Mary instructed Miriam in the Inner Channel, as shown in Plate One.

When Mary's friend died in 1958, Mary built a wing on Violet's house and moved in. This extension was connected at Miriam's room, and they essentially had a house to themselves. As Edith had earlier added on to this same house, for a brief time Mary, Miriam, Edith and Violet all lived under the same roof, until Edith's death in 1960. At that time the living room of her apartment was turned into a permanent classroom where Mary and

Miriam taught classes several times a week. Since Miriam had given up ceramics in the mid-fifties to devote more time to spiritual pursuits, she painted in oils for pleasure and profit and taught an art class once a week as well. Mary and Miriam soon became so busy with increased numbers of students and more classes that when Constance wanted to talk to her mother she would telephone, as it was the only way to get her undivided attention. The household was back to the old family tradition of cooking for a multitude. Classes always ended with coffee, tea, dessert and lively conversation. The classes continued to expand, and people returned year after year. In addition, Mary and Miriam created the first correspondence course in "Creative Color Analysis".

One of the private but ongoing parts of Mary's life was her association with the Dead Sea Scrolls. As was mentioned earlier, Mary read Latin, Greek, Ancient Hebrew, Aramaic and Sanskrit and had made an extensive study of Egyptology. Sometime after 1947, a bonded messenger began to appear at her door from time to time, leaving packages consisting of photographs of pieces with writing on them. She never showed them to family members or talked about what was happening until later. She would spend time alone in her room, working, and the messenger would come again and take the initial contents and her interpretations. In this way she read and translated many pieces of the Scrolls over a period of years. She later told those close to her about her work but never elaborated on the details except to explain that with an ancient language there may be more than one interpretation to a given passage. All interpretations submitted to committee were examined and those which appeared most accurate and consistent were chosen.

In 1971, Violet died, and this event was to re-shape the lives of many people associated with Mary. It became impossible for Violet's heirs to keep the property in South Pasadena, and in 1972 Mary and Miriam were told to start looking for other quarters. In October of that year, a group of friends formed a partnership to purchase an apartment complex in Santa Monica. Within a few months a dozen of the units were occupied by Mary's relatives, friends, or students. Mary and Miriam held classes just as before, this time in a large converted garage adjoining their apartment. New people were attracted to the group. Miriam, always an artist, converted a weed patch outside Mary's window into a lovely flower garden for her to enjoy.

One of the elements which changed the focus of Mary's work was that during the years in South Pasadena a group of students continued to attend classes for longer periods and with greater commitment to furthering her work than had been the case in the past. They began to know each other well, and a group connectedness took place. A number of these students were members of the Church of Ataraxia, which had been incorporated in 1942. The church is now known as The Essene Fellowship of Peace, since "ataraxia" is a Greek word for "peace", and the Essene philosophy is an integral part of Jesus' teaching and the thread that runs through Mary's teaching. Mary trained some of the more serious students as certified teachers, and some were ordained as ministers in this Fellowship.

Mary saw the Essenes as a positive model for living and Jesus' connection with them to be a natural Judeo-Christian bridge of consciousness. The group which formed itself around her in the 1960's and 1970's began to model its values in the Essene manner and to see its place in the world as that of one of the connectors between the earth plane and higher states of consciousness. This approach to Christianity was a spiritual one rather than religious.

Several of these students were of similar age and interested in choosing a place where they could live and learn in close proximity to each other. In the late 1970's they asked Mary if she would go with them if they found a compatible location. She reluctantly agreed. Her lifelong hesitancy to be put in a position of "leader" or "founder of a movement" made her hesitate to be the focal point of this undertaking. One of the group moved to Hemet, California, and "happened on" a ranch for sale near San Jacinto. It was an unusual place, abutting an Indian Reservation and considered sacred ground by the Indians. It had been used by a succession of religious groups in a variety of ways since the 1940's when the original owner donated it to the Catholic Bishopric of San Diego, which sent a group of nuns to live there.

Neither Hemet nor San Jacinto was a location where any of the members had expected to live. However, after several Fellowship members experienced a series of dreams and visions, all strikingly similar, they went to take a look. There was the house they had seen, a big stucco structure with a cross on top. It looked like something from a Gothic novel. A cottage, mobile home, library and crafts building and a half finished ten-bedroom dormitory completed the collection of buildings. There were liveoak trees near the buildings, and around the whole cluster were two hundred and sixty-five acres of mountains covered with chaparral. The only usable exit from the property was one narrow road out to a county road then on through the reservation. The ranch was purchased and named the Singing Heart Ranch. For several years it was home to the Essene Fellowship. Some lived full time, others visited, but all partook of the warmth and commitment of a shared life style based on love and each individual's desire to strive toward the "Christ Consciousness".

Those years were the last of Mary's life. Miriam's nursing skills, which had been called upon often throughout their association, became indispensable. Mary loved the old house and most of all the delicate sunrises and glorious sunsets, which backlit the hills in such a way that it seemed as if the sun were setting in all directions. She retreated more and more into her private self, and Miriam continued the classes with help from former students, now graduate teachers. They held Fellowship services, workshops on Color and retreats. There were Saturday night potlucks as well as weddings, holiday dinners and other events a big family shares.

By 1980, the year of Mary's death, the average age of the membership coupled with the enormous physical work needed to maintain a ranch of that size, proved to be beyond the residents' capacity. In 1981 the Ranch was sold. The members moved into Hemet and San Jacinto, disbanding the group living arrangement but maintaining the classes and meditation meetings in each other's homes.

The legacy left by Dr. George, Mary and Miriam is a lesson in unconditional love. Mary walked in the light of faith through all of her days. It was no coincidence that her favorite colors were purple and rose; faith and love were the cornerstones of her existence. One of the characteristics of Mary as a teacher was that she believed and lived that which came authentically and personally from her own experience. She encouraged her students to do the same. She never had the desire to lead, direct or be idolized, only to show quietly by example what love of God and living in Creative Color had meant to her. The teachers often pressed her for "how to's" and uniform teaching methods. Her reply was, "Color is my way. If it means something to you, go forth and teach it in your own way, but never change the definitions.[2] If you desire to lead a more balanced life, to accomplish certain goals, to develop spiritually or to make changes in your life, Color can play a large part in accomplishing these things. I would add that Color has a spiritual source. Jesus said, 'I am the light of the world.' Color is light revealed — vibration, energy, the visible essence of the life force. It is a catalyst or change agent. It is safe, and it protects."

The balance of this book has been compiled to assist those seekers who may be interested in Creative Color as a tool for growth. The presentation will go from the scientific perspective on light and color to its spiritual manifestation; from the visual presentation of the Color Fans (or Arcs) and the written meanings of these colors to directions on how to make use of this knowledge. Included are writings by Mary, Dr. George and Miriam on various aspects of Color and the philosophy by which it was taught. This gives the reader the opportunity to share their faith, love and unique vision of this colorful world in which we live.

---

[2] The "meanings" as printed near the Color Plates are Mary's "definitions".

Chapter 2

COLOR AND MAN

> It is recognized that out beyond the spectrum of physical sight there exists a large realm of stimuli that, had we the organism to react to it, many things which today are unknown would become common knowledge.
>
> Out beyond these that induce the sense of sight are waves that are more intense and more frequent, but as far as man is concerned they may as well be non-existent, for he perceives them not.
>
> Mary D. Weddell

The goal of this book is to help man perceive more of the "large realm of stimuli" unprocessed by man's current sensory equipment. Some of those intangibles are the invisible skeletal reality for all in the universe. The content of this book is derived from those invisible realms and is designed to help this visible world. The meanings and energies of color are the medium of communication.

Color is the language of light, the light that permeates our bodies and our world. Color imbues the planet below and the heavens above — the pink roses, the verdant trees, the reds and oranges in a sunset, the marvelous soft blues and grays mingled with lilac beyond a sky of billowing clouds. Man lives in a universe powerfully designed by color. As energy it is both visible and invisible. Color envelops him. Man cannot separate himself from it. Light and color permeate his being, and he, in turn, radiates an essence that sparkles like the night sky filled with stars. It is no accident that the ancients spoke often of man as the microcosm of God's marcrocosmic world.

What is color? It is all that we see and more. Each person sees and uses it uniquely. Many yearn to understand it more. It is seen differently and described differently from many points of view.

Scientists know color as the sensation resulting from stimulation of the retina of the eye by light waves of certain lengths or, color as a measurable vibration in the electromagnetic spectrum. As such it is studied and used as an energy. Because different colors are the result of energy as matter moving with varying speeds and creating varying densities, color is one verification of the phenomenon of the motion of matter. Physics recognizes color as both an energy vibration and a pulsing wave of motion. As energy in motion, color travels through the universe at all levels, and it can act as a catalyst or change agent at all levels. This, man is recognizing as he strives to use color in motivational ways in his life. For example, psychologists will advise warm or cool colors for different purposes.

Artists have always been sensitive to the myriad hues of color, often including the golden nimbus around a saint's head to indicate the inner essence emerging. Doctors are using color in some healing situations and have seen a light leave the human being at death, measured the energy essence lost at that moment, and concluded that this was man's soul essence.[3] Kirlian photography and other devices are measuring and recording more and more color variables in the auric field of energy surrounding man. Thus, are the professionals in many specialties beginning to prove the concepts held by mystics for centuries. As the many viewpoints merge in the twentieth century perhaps much that was known and practiced for the benefit of mankind will again be viable.

Mary Weddell bridged these varying concepts of color by terming her students "colorists", those who study and use color. The emphasis was two-fold: as a power to assist a person in self-therapy and soul-expansion, and as an energy catalyst for healing self and others or life situations. Mary's revealed color meanings evolved into a "Color Dictionary" of color definitions she had received inspirationally. In her mystical experiences these concepts of color were verified. Thus, color emerged as a "silent language".

Mary taught that color is a communication tool, a means of understanding between man and his Creator, and it is man's challenge to be a "co-creator with God" in its responsible use. In the past man used many symbolic ways to share ideas. Man first communicated by gestures and sounds, and these are still used today by coaches and athletes or as the basis of the two sign language systems of the deaf.

Man next communicated by verbal and written word symbols. Solidified into printed text, these form the base of the print mass communication industry which is rapidly being surpassed by electronic communication devices, utilizing sight and sound symbols. Sound can become music, at certain frequencies, giving easement and inspiration to every culture in the unique style, rhythm and beat of its choice. Color can do the same. It is recognized that each sound has a color and each color a sound. Used together, as they often are, color and sound can become man's most powerful energy and communication stimuli.

Color, as a silent communication tool, can be used to convey meaning between man and his Creator, man and man, and man and his inner self. When used as a method of sharing knowledge, Color becomes the language which bridges the higher dimensions of sensed reality with the reality sensed in the physical dimension. Thus man has grasped this insight when he speaks of casting "great light" of understanding on matters, or asks to be "enlightened" with greater truths, to be brought forth from the shadows of darkness and ignorance into the brilliant blaze of illumined new knowledge. As man learns to bring meaning from higher dimensions to his material environment, many think, heaven will be brought to earth. By understanding and using color, man will be arrayed in the "full armor of God".

---

[3] Alexis Carrel "Man The Unknown."

Color, as the language of light, is visible when it expresses in the physical plane of light. In its higher, auric vibration it expresses invisibly in the higher spans of the spectrum. Color will be discussed in this book in many octaves of light — as used in the physical world and as a spiritual expression of man's soul. As the student of Color perseveres and becomes a practicing colorist, his spiritual gifts are developed until the extended colors of the higher dimensions are seen and the meanings recognized. The seeker recognizes the great trust involved in using the powerful color rays and accepts the responsibility of their use. These color messages of love and wisdom strengthen the seeker so that he is able to assist others in the highest form of brotherly love — to walk the path of spiritual evolution together.

Man's concept of a god has varied from material images to those of a Creator embodying Light and Love and Intelligence as the macrocosm of our world. We, as particles of this essence and energy, sons of God, particles of Light, can accept a newer system of communication — Color — as we now accept that, indeed, we are pulsating particles of energy like the chairs we sit on or the plants and animals we love. We can accept ourselves as part of a vibrating electric universe which is the universe as man now knows it, and we can accept that that universe expresses in sound and color, as man is now proving. This is that "heaven on earth" promised and so longed for that man almost despairs of its ever arriving. But, he need not, for it is _he_ who can build this heavenly kingdom. And, the language of Color can be the architect.

As in any other building, precision is the standard. So, too, with color used as a language to communicate or as a therapeutic energy. Color divides into tints and hues. Each has a specific vibration, and the meanings of some are known. To adhere to the correct meaning, the correct color symbol must be used. However, color perception will vary among individuals. There is a range of acceptability. Just as the letter "A" can be written "A" or "a" and still be communicating accurately, so, too, can some colors vary and still be described by the same meaning. But, should the letter "a" look more like "e, o, or u" comprehension has changed. So, too, with color if deviation is too great. It requires a trained eye and one skilled in Color language to judge allowable levels of variation. As verbal language begins with one letter and expands to syllables, words, sentences, pages, etc., so, too, do different color combinations expand in meaning.

Language, whether spoken or printed, can be used to hurt or help, to incite or to soothe. So too with the color language. Color uses the visual sensory system to convey meaning and travels on the more rapid wave-lengths of the visible and invisible frequencies of the spectrum. Color has potent and far-reaching effects. High frequency sound and high intensity laser beams are now recognized and used with great care by the medical profession. So too must the practicing colorist responsibly use color combinations which can help himself or another. Since color travels through the universe at all levels, it can act as a catalyst or change agent at all levels.

It has been said that matter is light trapped by gravity. This, then, would apply to color. As earlier stated color is one verification of the phenomenon of the motion of matter. Color shows how light is absorbed, because it would be moving at a rate beyond which the denser and slower matter could reflect or absorb. If particles of matter are disturbed so as to move too slowly or too quickly in all or parts of the whole, the light, or color, energy would reflect this difference by a change in tone or hue. If additional color energy could be applied to the imbalanced area, or whole, a change could conceivably be made. This is the basis of much current research into the therapeutic use of color, whether applied mechanically or through human visualization. This is the change available daily as man perceives color, for all creation is filled with glorious colors which delight the eye and give zest to living.

Man is a colorful entity. One needs only to consider hair, eyes, skin, bones, blood and nerves to see a wide spectrum of colors. Since man is a colorful being and sensitively responsive to change, the application of suitable colors can, indeed, be beneficial to his growth in wholeness and balance. This is the restorative function of the universal color rays described in this book. The psychological and spiritual meaning of color can be a means of clarifying self-knowledge and of changing life for the better, providing a means to inner understanding of oneself and others by awakening the intuitive nature. Applied rightly, Color establishes harmonious relationships with others, awakens one's faculties to greater spiritual reality and integrates the whole man in balanced growth.

Color can enhance power of prayer and can still the mind in preparation for meditation. In illness of mind, emotions or body, modern thinking has finally caught up with ancient thought, for history records repetitive cycles of color use. Through the analysis of the Color Rays and their application to life, the colorist develops a realization of the oneness of all and the helpfulness of living consciously in the rhythm of the laws of the universe.

Daily, man receives from the universe, yet is unaware of the gifts. Who has not admired a sunset or awakened to the glory of a sunrise sky? Here one receives a color treatment from the Great Source of Life — the silvery blue lavender of tranquility, the rosy peach of gratitude, the soft seafoam green of awareness, the soft pink-lavender of inspiration or the more smoky pink-lavender-blue of humility. These and more are seen in the morning or evening sky. Is energy needed? Look up at the vast blue sky or walk barefoot in the grass and be renewed. Breathe in the fragrance of the garden, the faith of the purple violets, and the glorious shell pink blossoms of the peach tree in bloom. Feel God's love about you. All is provided, one needs only to become aware of it.

Throughout the ages artists have depicted a golden halo surrounding the heads of saints, sometimes expanding it to a nimbus of light around a person. This entire field of color, or aura, has recently been under scientific scrutiny but has long been known and referred to in mystical writings. It is now sometimes called the bioplasmic body, or the electromagnetic field. (See Diagram 1.)

This pulsing, ever-spiraling life energy emanates from the divine center within. The radiant energy flows from this center through every part of man's body, extending beyond the body and under the feet. The aura may extend only a short distance from the body. This usually occurs when there is little soul attainment or when energy is depleted. Clairvoyants have seen it extending to quite a distance, equally on all sides. Scientists have described it as "light radiating from the body in the form of photons"[4] and have recorded this energy moving at up to 200,000 cycles per second. According to Dr. Valerie Hunt, "part of the aura is within the hearing range" and she has "six or seven-hundred times recorded the sound" of the aura. Additional work is being done on recording the sounds of colors and the colors of sounds.

---

[4] This and subsequent quotations in this paragraph are from Valerie Hunt, D. Ed., Professor Emeritus, Department of Kinesiology, University of California at Los Angeles, radio interview, March 22, 1986. Quoted by permission.

THE RELATIONSHIP OF THE INNER CHANNEL TO MAN'S AURA

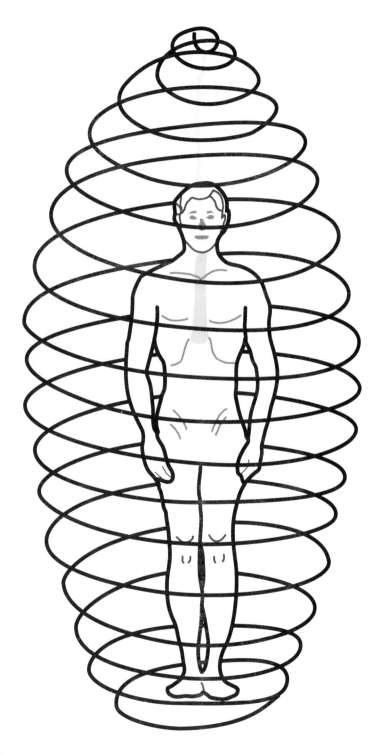

Copyright © 1984 by Miriam B. Willis to illustrate the ORIGINAL COURSE IN CREATIVE COLOR ANALYSIS by Mary Dies Weddell. International copyright secured. Made in U.S.A. All rights reserved.

When one is well developed spiritually, the aura contains almost all the colors and tints there are. Dr. Hunt terms such an aura containing the whole spectrum of color a "coherent field". She also said that she believes that this energy field is the primary communicator between living species.

People, often unknowingly, affect each other through their auras. One often hears, "The chemistry between us is right." When two auras are harmonious, the chemistry is right. When inharmonious, discord can result. One person strongly filled with love, peace, harmony and kindliness can exert a calming influence on an entire group of people by merely being present. As Miriam Willis taught in her classes, there are no spaces in the aura, but between the colors are silvery lighted bands which separate the colors and "feed" them. These bands make it easier for an advanced reader of auras to distinguish its many separate colors.

Miriam also taught that permanent rays are developed in the aura as man grows spiritually and is able to sustain those qualities of spirit that ennoble the character. But, she would point out, even permanent rays differ among persons, depending on the life purpose and the life opportunities. For example, the rays of some individuals express brotherhood, kindness and charity. Other individuals may express purity of purpose, faith and humility. However, all such qualities bring spiritual balance and are permanently registered in the auric field. These permanent rays are visible to the reader of auras and tell him the measure of the height of the soul's development. Permanent rays developed in previous lifetimes are displayed only when the individual unerringly expresses them in this life. If not consciously used in the current life they will flash only occasionally in the aura. The rays of an old soul will appear, however, signaling the true potential of the individual.

As Mary explained, within the framework of these permanent rays in the aura of the highly developed person are myriads of colors revealing each individual's special gifts and talents, personality traits, habits and dispositional patterns of thinking. The aura of a spiritually developed master displays a balanced synthesis of permanent rays, fully expressed, and the high attainments of his individual destiny. Indeed and in truth, the developed master "lives and moves and has his being" in his great all-enveloping Creator, whose loving power feeds and sustains the whole of life, redeeming and restoring, strengthening and making whole with infinite patience those who seek to become perfect in Him.

The aura is both a record of the individual's past and a constantly changing picture of his current condition. Man is continually creating color through his thoughts, his emotions, his health, his intellectual and spiritual achievements. Such states of mind and emotion are reflected in the emanations of etheric substance from his life center.

Because the colors in one's aura automatically change as one's thoughts and emotions change, it is possible to eliminate old habit patterns and unwanted traits by changing the thoughts and emotions. This is more easily said than done. Since the root causes of emotional responses lie in the subconscious, changing them deliberately can be extremely difficult. A simple, effective way is to add desired, needed traits and qualities by applying to one's own God-center the colors which will gently modify, absorb and clear the old conditions and replace them with beneficial ones. By flooding the aura with the virtues that will sweep away the undesirable traits, one also becomes more conscious of one's thoughts and learns to be in charge of them.

The changes brought through Creative Color are spiritually activated and are usually gradual. They progress from the spiritual body to the mental and emotional bodies. Lastly, they take effect in the physical body. It is far easier to heal a difficulty before it crystalizes in the physical than it is to heal a physical impairment. Because the progression of healing from the spiritual level to the physical is usually slow, and because color applications are very gentle, applications often require repetition. When the spirit is healed, the physical healing which follows is likely to be permanent. Some people can diagnose by seeing or sensing the aura just as Mary and Dr. George did decades ago. With appropriate color application the threatening condition can be healed before it manifests in the physical body as dis-ease.

Many times healings of physical problems occur in a large gathering. Sometimes they prove to be temporary. Perhaps the consciousness of the one healed was essentially unprepared to accept the changes even though the desire for healing may have seemed sincere, or the person could not maintain the necessary high state of balanced awareness for a long enough period of time for the healing to permeate all his bodies. Color is the sustaining force for balanced awareness that can catalyze long-lasting results.

Since the aura is the garment of spirit, it is linked to the great universal currents and is affected by them, consciously or unconsciously. Herein lies the key to the secrets of the mysteries. For within the aura and lying in front of the solar plexus is the Inner Channel, the seat of the soul. Its function, as this central point, is the distribution of soul energy which is constantly regenerating the body in order to integrate man's physical, mental, emotional and spiritual aspects of being. This integration permits the manifestation, through the human vehicle, of God's love, wisdom and will expressed through joy, beauty, healing and understanding in love for mankind.

The Channel, heart and balancing force of the aura, is composed of etheric substance reaching up from the solar plexus through the crown of the head. At first, before the spiritual man awakens, it is like a capsule which can be compared to the single seed of a mighty tree. This capsule needs nourishment and the opportunity to begin to grow, which it does only as man prayerfully uses it. As the capsule expands from the God-center, its energy forms the Channel, which spirals upward through the top of the head.

The Channel's rate of vibration is the fastest in the human body. Its vibrating energy is a point of contact between man and his Creator. When this contact is consciously open, one experiences, in joy and gratitude, an ever-present sensitivity to the God presence. The developed Channel is active whether one is awake or asleep. It operates on a spiritual level at a frequency safely above the psychic field. One is never exposed to negative forces while in the Channel. The daily use of the Color Channel[5] activates further spiritual enlightenment, gives protection against the vibrations of the psychic field, deepens insight, helps to refine and balance the chakras of the endocrine system and thus the emotions, and helps to develop spiritual sight and hearing.

When we begin to climb this Inner Channel of our being (Plate 1), we start by standing in the color of the royal purple of faith, the unadulterated God-power by which we step into the unknown, assured by that faith that the God-power will sustain us and overcome our fears and lack of trust.

---

[5] Refer to Chapter 4 for detailed instructions in use of the Channel.

The gray lavender endows us with the patience needed for balanced growth through the influence of the Christ spirit represented by the silvery overlay.

The pink lavender of inspiration is related to the uplift and joy of traveling the spiritual path as we bring inspirational ideas into operation.

The rose lavender of the spiritual voice represents the light of conscience, the inner voice which reveals us to ourselves.

The blue orchid of prophecy tells us what we may become, a forth-telling, interpreting the revelation that comes as we listen to the inner voice.

The yellow bridge enlightens and lifts us to the rose orchid of the message bearer so that we can bring through the message from the higher dimensions, as the red lilac of the holding force for the band of Teachers sustains the higher power, releasing earth's spiritual power to meet this higher power.

Again, enlightenment uplifts us, this time to the union of mind and spirit, creating a balance to free the intellect to become the recording instrument of the spirit.

The light blue orchid develops in us the spirit of brotherhood and brings the great Invisible Brotherhood to our consciousness. It awakens the love-nature of man, the selfless love of the brotherhood of all mankind.

The expression of this higher octave of love results in the blush orchid of serenity. With it self-centeredness vanishes in the lightest green of desirelessness. Then, is the rose bisque of grace a gift of God, His perfume.

The light blue lavender of peace is the "peace that passeth all understanding".

In a letter to a friend, Dr. George Weddell wrote that peace is the perfect blending of the entire universe into one harmonious whole, without a single dissenting atom. He went on, "Peace means a perfect love and a perfect understanding, an abiding light that will shine in all dark places. No sorrow or misunderstanding can abide with peace. No turmoil is so great that this magic word does not turn the whitecaps of trouble into low waves of unrest which are succeeded by a beautiful calm where the weary soul finds rest."

And so the study and practice of Creative Color through the Inner Channel is a mystical journey toward development of the soul.

As Dr. George and Mary wrote, "The human aura is defined as the Kingdom of the Soul, color the key to the Channel. Color opens the way to self-unfoldment, to self-effacement and to self-discipline. It is the way of mental illumination and intuitive perception.

"The wise man makes the world his own initiation chamber, life itself the threshold of the mysteries. If a man can really command himself perfectly he can command all else. Those who would make true progress should look on every thing that happens to them in life as an initiation trial and so become, as it were, their own initiators. <u>Initiation is the revelation of love expressing itself in wisdom.</u>

"Along the path of development the seeker arrives at a mesa of universal consciousness. As he observes the signposts he reads 'This way alone'. At this point, great stress is laid on outer conditions. The mastery of pride, the control of appetite and desires are the first important steps and one needs guidance for he must depend upon his intellect. His mind can lead him into many bypaths, for appearances are deceiving.

"Sometimes a man at this stage seems insincere and vascillating. Eventually through trial and error and the love of the universal path, man is once again the seeker. Then his intellectual supremacy wanes while soul consciousness assumes domination. This is the first high point along the way. Symbol of the second state, he is given through the Creative Color Channel a vision nourished in the heart. He begins the assimilation of spiritual truth and the illumined power to use his intuitions in the conquest of his emotional nature.

"There are no physical limitations to inner vision. The spiritual faculties of man know no barriers of space nor time. A world of marvelous phenomena awaits his command. Within the natural but unused functions of the mind are dormant powers which can bring about a transformation of one's life.

As man continues to use the Color Channel he is taught to follow distinct zones of color and sound in order to be able to respond to the manifold activities in these zones. Because we know these auric minglings are inseparably connected with the universal auric ether, one sees them play in the creative and receptive ethers in which one is polarized.

"Color and sound become easy to interpret after one becomes familiar with auric colors, and by meditation or states of vision one has fully expressed one's spiritual powers to see. The next thing is to know and understand what one sees."

Through the study of Creative Color this is made possible. The following pages present the core of this teaching. The development of the seeker is bounded only by the limits he himself places upon it.

And the light blue lavender of Peace

To the rose bisque of Grace

Over the bridge of lightest green in Desirelessness

The blush orchid of Serenity

The light blue orchid of Brotherhood

To the glowing peach of Union of Mind and Spirit

Over the bridge of yellow Enlightenment

And the red lilac of the Holding Force for the Band of Teachers

To the rose orchid of the Message Bearer

Over the bridge of yellow Enlightenment

The blue orchid of Prophecy

The rose lavender of the Spiritual Voice

The pink lavender of Inspiration

And mount to the gray lavender of the Holding Force of Patience

I stand in the royal purple of Faith

The Inner Channel

Plate One

Copyright © 1984 by Miriam B. Willis to illustrate the ORIGINAL COURSE IN CREATIVE COLOR ANALYSIS by Mary Dies Weddell. International copyright secured. Made in U.S.A. All rights reserved.

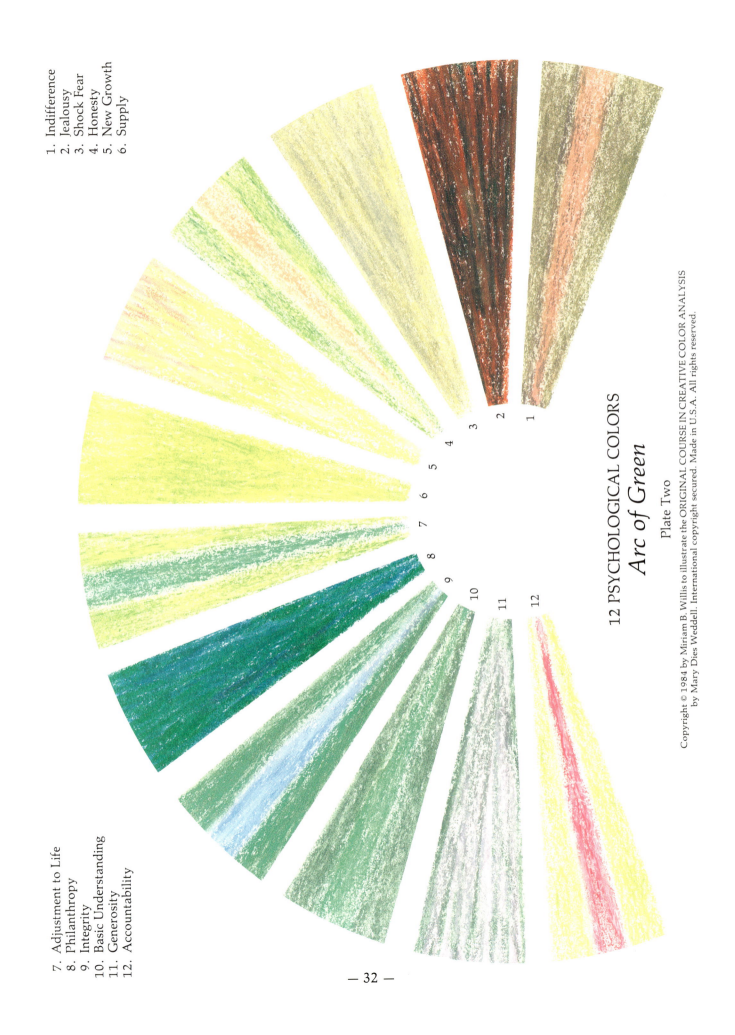

12 PSYCHOLOGICAL COLORS
Arc of Red

Plate Five

1. Heroic Courage
2. Hatred
3. Lust
4. Anger
5. Greed
6. Creative Life Force
7. Love
8. Joy
9. Friendship
10. Honor
11. Pride
12. Aggression

Copyright © 1984 by Miriam B. Willis to illustrate the ORIGINAL COURSE IN CREATIVE COLOR ANALYSIS by Mary Dies Weddell. International copyright secured. Made in U.S.A. All rights reserved.

Color Prayers

To Overcome Criticism

To Reduce Tension

Plate Six

Copyright © 1984 by Miriam B. Willis to illustrate the ORIGINAL COURSE IN CREATIVE COLOR ANALYSIS by Mary Dies Weddell. International copyright secured. Made in U.S.A. All rights reserved.

The Lord's Prayer in Color

Plate Seven

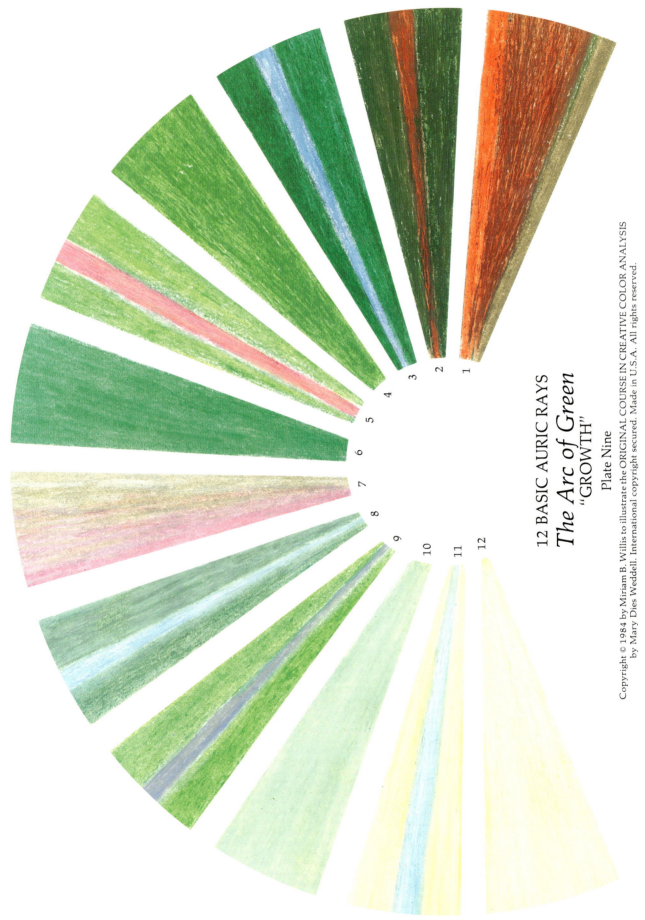

Color Descriptions and Meanings
The Arc of Green — "Growth"

1st RAY: **Dark Green and Dull Grayish Brown, Orange at Left Side**
Meaning: The color at base of the aura in which man stands. When seen higher in the aura, it denotes sluggish indifference to spiritual development, disinterest in general, sloth. Orange at left side denotes self assertion.

2nd RAY: **Dark Olive Green, Dark Henna Orange Midray**
Meaning: Fundamental righteousness, zealous, self centered, stubborn opinions.

3rd RAY: **Dark Forest Green, Blue Midray**
Meaning: Foundational balance, poise, stability, fairminded.

4th RAY: **Grass Green**
Meaning: Reality of life, acceptance of life's challenges.

5th RAY: **Green Yellow, Old Rose Midray**
Meaning: Vibrant universal force, entering higher consciousness, flexible, open-minded.

6th RAY: **Blue Tinted Emerald Green**
Meaning: Spiritual life present in the physical, sign of rebirth.

7th RAY: **Silvered Olive Green, Overtone of Old Rose to the Left**
Meaning: Denotes age of soul. The older soul has more old rose overtone.

8th RAY: **Moss Green, Light Blue Gray Midray**
Meaning: Hidden development, a sign to the teacher that student has what it takes.

9th RAY: **Apple Green, Blue Midray**
  Meaning: Conscious of immaturity, mental or spiritual opinions strong.

10th RAY: **Seafoam Green**
  Meaning: Awareness of sowing and reaping, the Law of Compensation, receptive, alert, expanding in conscious understanding.

11th RAY: **Light Yellow Green, Soft Light Blue Midray**
  Meaning: Act of at-one-ment with Self, responsibility taken, a measure of peace, joy of accomplishment.

12th RAY: **Delicate Yellow Green**
  Meaning: At-one-ment with God, illumination, path made clear through self control.

FROM THE ORIGINAL COURSE IN CREATIVE COLOR ANALYSIS BY MARY DIES WEDDELL

Color Descriptions and Meanings
The Arc of Yellow — "Illumination"

1st RAY: **Brown Mustard**
<u>Meaning</u>: Strong opinions, very set, self asserting and dominating, at times benevolent and wise. They make good teachers. Their domination is modified by 1st ray of red (potential power, testing ground of faith).

2nd RAY: **Golden Yellow Ochre, Bit of Flame**
<u>Meaning</u>: A soul old in experience, often tested and found to be over confident, loathes to be corrected, standing on premise of having all knowledge.

3rd RAY: **Light Yellow Green with Buff Streaks**
<u>Meaning</u>: A natural ray for accumulation, drawing all things to the self and in turn doling them out sparingly.

4th RAY: **Canary Yellow**
<u>Meaning</u>: Life consciously identified with spiritual principles, endeavoring to keep integrated by Spirit, earnestly trying.

5th RAY: **Five Colors (Right to Left): Pink Orchid, Deep Rose, Pale Yellow, Tangerine and Brown**
<u>Meaning</u>:
- **Pink Orchid** . . . . Reveals man is on quest of Spirit
- **Deep Rose** . . . . Asking forgiveness
- **Pale Yellow** . . . . Shows rebirth
- **Tangerine** . . . . Man faced by habits of the past
- **Brown** . . . The steep and rugged path he must overcome

6th RAY: **Silvery Blue White, Pale Yellow Underlay**
<u>Meaning</u>: A living ray, permanent, seen in all auras, often called "the silver cord", attenuated when out of the body, severed only at death.

7th RAY: Four Colors (Right to Left): Yellow Orange, Rose, Pastel Rose, Pale Yellow
Meaning: This ray reveals the source of supply to the aura. Within this ray there is an orb which is very pale yellow or richer sun yellow, according to the spiritual development of the person. This is the ray one looks for first in reading an aura. This is the source of supply of light or illumination to the aura. Its location also indicates the degree of development attained.

8th RAY: Peach Pink
Meaning: A warm nature, keen to follow a leader, kindly and often self sacrificing.

9th RAY: Apricot Pink
Meaning: A soul naturally filled with the love of life, of mankind, a type easily developed.

10th RAY: (Right to Left): Deep Rose to Flesh
Meaning: Denoting one who has the capacity for loving, has broken many habits, broken old molds of thinking, walks the way of love, tempered by Spirit, is temperate in all things, able to judge truly because he has learned to judge himself truly. He respects himself and all men.

11th RAY: Rich Sun Yellow
Meaning: Action of maturity, converts nature to spiritual expression toward fellow man. This soul has sought through many channels of church and cult, etc. His nebulous ideas have become synchronized into a force unifying himself with the Christ within.

12th RAY: Sunset (Right to Left): Flame Pink to Yellow
Meaning: A God ray of a developed person, many times seen and described as gold about a person.

FROM THE ORIGINAL COURSE IN CREATIVE COLOR ANALYSIS BY MARY DIES WEDDELL

Color Descriptions and Meanings
The Arc of Red — "Metamorphosis"

1st RAY: **Light Orange Yellow Center, Rose Orange at Sides**
  Meaning: Potential power, the testing ground of faith, field of realization and overcoming.

2nd RAY: **Scarlet and Orange**
  Meaning: Holds anger and its derivatives: quick anger, pride of opinion, self glorification, exaggeration and criticism.

3rd RAY: **Three Merging Colors: Soft Red, Soft Green and Soft Yellow**
  Meaning: Life force expressed by Spirit, merging of the three bodies (physical, red), (mental, green), and (spiritual, yellow). Such an one speaks the truth without exaggeration.

4th RAY: **Red, Purple, Maroon and Yellow**
  Meaning: Higher forces entering the Path, shows one on the Path of Christ Jesus, willing to lay down the "old man," ready for the "new", twice born.

5th RAY: **(Right to Left): Deep Red, Brown Streak, Rose Red**
  Meaning: Christ's way, the struggle of forty days in the wilderness, viewing the emotions. Here truth of self is revealed and man desires to do something about it. Deep cleansing, learning of Him, following. The ray of conversion.

6th RAY: **(Right to Left): Rose Red to Coral Pink**
  Meaning: Clear thinking and pure purpose. This is the first ray of wisdom, promise of spiritual sight, dreams and visions will begin to be comprehended.

7th RAY: **Salmon Pink, Deep Rose Midray**
Meaning: Bespeaks a soul seeking, has great power for development, perseverance, desire to share, could become a teacher.

8th RAY: **Plum, Red and Yellow**
Meaning: Determination to follow the spiritual way, balanced enthusiasm, energy directed Godward, carries his load willingly, happy and content.

9th RAY: **Light Rose and Light Blue**
Meaning: Selflessness, has overcome bigotry, shows one developing on the Path, Christ centered life.

10th RAY: **Coral Rose, Flesh Pink Center**
Meaning: A nature resplendent in warmth and the virtues of kindness, considerate and thoughtful of others' needs, talent for making the best of things.

11th RAY: **Pink**
Meaning: Tenderness and concern for a brother, steps in the shade that others may shine, no desire to star.

12th RAY: **Soft Grayed Old Rose**
Meaning: A universal concept of life, tolerant with understanding, seeing God in all creation, recognizing the One Source in manifold form and color and degree of creative expression.

FROM THE ORIGINAL COURSE IN CREATIVE COLOR ANALYSIS BY MARY DIES WEDDELL

Chapter 3

CORE OF COLOR KNOWLEDGE

> As the sun is the lens through which the energy of God flows to give physical life to all creation, so the soul of man is the lens through which the energy of God flows to feed his spiritual growth and unfoldment. Thus man reflects all that he is in the color emanations of his aura.
>
> Miriam B. Willis

Can you imagine a straightforward, simple presentation of the most complex concepts man has to deal with? Have you ever ardently wished or asked for an explanation of love, for instance? Human love, the Christ love, generosity, peace? These concepts are energies and their purest form is in color seen in light. This chapter will enable you to see, in color, as nearly as possible, representations of such ethereal energies, and in Chapter 4 you will learn how to use these colors to heal and bless yourself and others.

These arcs of color, in fan shape, together with their original definitions and expanded meanings, are the heart and core of Creative Color. There are twelve Psychological and twelve Basic Spiritual, or Auric, rays in each of the colors green, blue, yellow and red and twelve Basic rays of the purple arc — one hundred and eight in all.

The color plates of the arcs and their original definitions highlight the chapter. Expanded meanings of all the rays are given. Then, the Balancing Force of the Purple Arc is discussed. Finally, an Analysis of the Relationships of the Basic Spiritual Rays is given. You, the reader, will be able to go at your own speed from the simple explanation to the complex and subtle nuances of ray meanings.

All colors are contained in light. In nature all are beautiful. In the emotional energy patterns of mankind, the beautiful can become distorted as well as the reverse. The rays which are designated in this book as "Psychological" reflect in man's aura the mental, emotional and physical expression of his day-to-day living. Some refer to them as the lower octave of light. These colors flash in his aura as his thoughts and moods change. They include both positive and negative rays. Some psychological rays stabilize man's life for good and prepare him for further awareness. Negative rays, if indulged, hinder and tend to hold him in undesirable conditions, revealing habitual faults. Positive rays persistently applied have power to transform or dissolve those undesirable conditions.

You may notice a similarity between some psychological and some spiritual rays. There is a difference between the similar colors, however, when they are seen in light instead of pigment. Spiritual rays have more luminosity. Many psychological rays help to activate the related spiritual qualities, and the spiritual qualities, in turn, increase the positive energy of the psychological rays. Each is essential to the other. Therefore, in any analysis and subsequent synthesis of the expansion of their meanings, overlapping is inevitable. The names of the psychological colors are familiar to many persons, who tend to absorb their meanings and values from early environmental influences and to accept them.

With spiritual development change occurs. The basic rays of the Spiritual Arcs, also referred to as a higher octave of light, provide both a standard by which to measure growth and the means of further development. The majority of these Auric Spiritual rays are those you are endeavoring to express in your life. Such qualities as selfless love, kindness and gratitude can move you toward the awakening of the Christ Consciousness and the principle of Universal Love.

Each of the spiritual arcs is concerned with the maturing of an essential portion of man's spiritual nature. Each spiritual arc has twelve steps of unfoldment. The first ray is foundational with some indication of adventure or enterprise plus ego strength to some degree. The twelfth ray is the culmination of the entire arc's meaning. Rarely does a person develop the rays in the order in which they are numbered. We come into each life with different missions, different problems to solve, different tests to overcome. One person may have thoroughly developed a ray in a previous life and have only to review it at this time. The same person might find it necessary to go over and over again the work of some other ray because of a recurring problem in his life. Each person's mission, tests and special abilities are uniquely his.

It is helpful to keep in mind the general meanings of the colors as the rays are studied. Therefore, a brief discussion of each of the five basic colors follows.

Green represents growth, energy, accumulation and, in its higher frequencies, heightened awareness. Greens are as necessary to man as they are to Nature. As in Nature, where from the palest green in the emerging sprout to the full richness of the mature dark green — and all the shades and tints between — a process of growth is taking place. Change and growth are an inevitable part of life. Clear greens help you to be flexible and to adapt to change so that growth proceeds naturally. To resist change is to hinder normal growth. Too much green accents the ego and creates imbalance. As is well known, moderation and balance are of prime importance for growth.

Blue. For clear understanding and richer realization of one's growth, guidance and training are needed. Blues aid this process by training the ego, or personality, through the development of positive attitudes that can overcome self-centeredness and negativity and by exertion of the will toward expression of these positive attitudes in daily living.

Blue is a cool color contributing to an overall condition of calmness and serenity. Various colors of blue are soothing to the nerves and can lead to spiritual awareness. The lighter colors of blue are healing, and the darker, or more intense, clear colors are positive forces that stimulate will power and right action. They give control and discipline, and the higher frequencies of blue continue this activity on a spiritual level. They guide the little ego toward a positive conscious use of controlled emotion, which is the foundation of spiritual power.

<u>Yellow</u> colors warm and uplift. Some stimulate the intellect and aid in assimilation of knowledge. Yellows throw light on the events, the relationships, the habit patterns of life, bringing a type of rebirth through enlightenment. The positive yellows are lights on the path of life. They strengthen mature action and lead to the illumination of the developed person — a conscious union with God, a realization of the Divine within. There are degrees of this intuitional awakening and many of the yellows mark the steps in growth.

<u>Red.</u> Red is a warm color that stimulates activity in life. It gives impetus to physical activity and catalyzes changes in consciousness. The slower vibrating frequencies indicate selfish intent, and result in distorted relationships whereas the positive tints and combinations contain numerous expressions of love. The higher frequencies of red give the enabling power to transform man's nature to express spiritual qualities. With such expression, man remembers more often that he is a spiritual being inhabiting an earthly body. They help to refine the human body-temple and to maintain a more subtle vibration so that the spirit within can function with greater ease. The natural environment of spirit is unconditional love.

<u>Purple.</u> Purples are concerned with balanced interaction, whether between oneself and one's Source or Creator, between persons or between oneself and the environment in which one lives. They balance all one's forces — physical, mental, emotional and spiritual — with the whole of life. Helpful to all the color rays, the Purples symbolize attributes of God and represent the true synthesis of all the best that man can be.

The organization of material in this chapter has been specifically designed to allow each individual to absorb this vital core of knowledge at a speed comfortable to him and to use it in a manner applicable to his own life situation.

Color Descriptions and Meanings*

PSYCHOLOGICAL RAYS OF GREEN

Plate 2

1st Ray: <u>Murky Green, Clouded Apricot Midray</u>
Meaning: Indifference

2nd Ray: <u>Orange Heavily Streaked with Dark Green</u>
Meaning: Jealousy

3rd Ray: <u>Grayed Yellow Green</u>
Meaning: Shock Through Fear

4th Ray: <u>Soft Yellow Green, Pink Apricot Midray</u>
Meaning: Honesty

5th Ray: <u>Yellow Green tipped with Light Red Rose Streaks</u>
Meaning: New Growth

6th Ray: <u>Chartreuse</u>
Meaning: Supply

7th Ray: <u>Yellow Green, Blue Green Midray</u>
Meaning: Adjustment to Life

8th Ray: <u>Deep Green, Touch of Blue Underlay</u>
Meaning: Philanthropy

9th Ray: <u>Gray Green, Grayed Cobalt Blue Midray</u>
Meaning: Integrity

10th Ray: <u>Gray Green, Blue Green Midray</u>
Meaning: Basic Understanding

11th Ray: <u>Gray Green with Lavender Streaks</u>
Meaning: Generosity

12th Ray: <u>Light Yellow Green, Coral Midray</u>
Meaning: Accountability

---

* These are Mary Weddell's original definitions. This note applies to all the pages where the word "Meaning" (or "Meanings") is used.

Color Descriptions and Meanings

PSYCHOLOGICAL RAYS OF BLUE

Plate 3

1st Ray: <u>Dark Blue, Streaks of Brown and Maroon</u>
Meaning: Evil Intent

2nd Ray: <u>Ashen Gray Blue</u>
Meaning: Fear

3rd Ray: <u>Deep Bright Blue</u>
Meaning: Reliability

4th Ray: <u>Deep Green Blue</u>
Meaning: Emotion

5th Ray: <u>Bright Blue, Grayed Cobalt Blue Midray</u>
Meaning: Moral Courage

6th Ray: <u>Three Colors: Right Side, Bright Leaf Green, Left Side, Light Blue-Green, Rose Midray</u>
Meaning: Justice

7th Ray: <u>Three Colors: Right Side, Cobalt Blue Lavender, Left Side, Rose Lavender with Blue, Chartreuse Midray</u>
Meaning: Ambition

8th Ray: <u>Light Bright Blue</u>
Meaning: Loyalty

9th Ray: <u>Bright Royal Blue, Rose Midray</u>
Meaning: Responsibility

10th Ray: <u>Royal Blue on the Right Side Shading to Light Lavender on the Left</u>
Meaning: Innate Refinement

11th Ray: <u>Soft Light Blue, Touch of Lavender</u>
Meaning: Life's Harmony

12th Ray: <u>Light Green Blue, Light Yellow Midray</u>
Meaning: Self-Analysis

Color Descriptions and Meanings

PSYCHOLOGICAL RAYS OF YELLOW

Plate 4

1st Ray: <u>Orange Streaked with Dark Brown and Dark Green</u>
Meaning: Deceit

2nd Ray: <u>Orange Streaked with Henna Brown and Dark Gray Green</u>
Meaning: Gossip

3rd Ray: <u>Medium Yellow Gray-Green, Yellow Ochre Midray Dirtied with Gray-Green</u>
Meaning: Cowardice

4th Ray: <u>Strong Orange Overlaid with Brown and Olive Green</u>
Meaning: Scandal

5th Ray: <u>Strong Orange</u>
Meaning: Desire

6th Ray: <u>Bright Yellow</u>
Meaning: Happiness

7th Ray: <u>Light Pink Orange</u>
Meaning: Appreciation

8th Ray: <u>Light Yellow, Coral Midray</u>
Meaning: Mental Peace

9th Ray: <u>Yellow with Soft Brown Overlay, Rich Yellow Midray</u>
Meaning: Steadfast Confidence

10th Ray: <u>Rosy Copper</u>
Meaning: Motivation

11th Ray: <u>Salmon Pink Overlaid with Burnt Sienna</u>
Meaning: Common Sense

12th Ray: <u>Rich Yellow, Touch of Pale Brown, Pale Coral Midray</u>
Meaning: Intellect

Color Descriptions and Meanings

PSYCHOLOGICAL RAYS OF RED

Plate 5

1st Ray: <u>Bright Red</u>
Meaning: Heroic Courage

2nd Ray: <u>Orange and Olive Green Heavily Overlaid with Intense Maroon Red</u>
Meaning: Hatred

3rd Ray: <u>Muddy Orange Green, Dirty Orange Midray</u>
Meaning: Lust

4th Ray: <u>Red Orange, Bright Red Midray</u>
Meaning: Anger

5th Ray: <u>Grayed Olive Green, Dirty Orange Midray</u>
Meaning: Greed

6th Ray: <u>Rich Rose Red</u>
Meaning: Creative Life Force

7th Ray: <u>Pink Rose Lightly Underlaid with Pale Orange</u>
Meaning: Love

8th Ray: <u>Light Salmon Pink</u>
Meaning: Joy

9th Ray: <u>Three Colors (Right to Left): Rose Pink, Orange Coral, Flesh Pink</u>
Meaning: Friendship

10th Ray: <u>Three Colors (Right to Left): Rich Rose Lavender, Bright Yellow, Deep Lavender Rose</u>
Meaning: Honor

11th Ray: <u>Soft Red Orange Streaked with Purple</u>
Meaning: Pride

12th Ray: <u>Three Colors (Right to Left): Rosy Salmon Pink, Sky Blue, Flesh Pink</u>
Meaning: Aggression

Expanded Meanings of the Psychological Rays

GREEN

Plate 2

1. <u>Indifference:</u> Murky Yellow Green, Clouded Apricot Midray

   This combination reveals disinterest and apathy. The soft apricot in the midray without the cloudy gray overlay will help to overcome indifference.

2. <u>Jealousy:</u> Orange Heavily Streaked with Dark Green

   In the psychological realm of the aura the intensity of the green energy and the orange of desire display a fearful and suspicious nature, often vindictive. The rays of love and generosity will help overcome jealousy.

3. <u>Shock Through Fear:</u> Grayed Yellow Green

   This color is quite apparent in one who has suffered a sudden startle, fright, or shock to the system. This type of fear diminishes the life force and creates a paralyzing effect in the entire body. The rich rose red ray of the creative life force proves restorative.

4. <u>Honesty:</u> Soft Yellow Green, Pink Apricot Midray

   The qualities of honesty are openness, sincerity, truthfulness, integrity and fairness. True honesty wants to reveal all, but the midray adds tact to frankness.

5. <u>New Growth:</u> Yellow Green Tipped with Light Red Rose Streaks

   This reveals new beginnings in consciousness. The growth process has been stimulated by the red rose streaks of the Creative Life Force, the intrinsic factor for life and growth.

6. <u>Supply:</u> Chartreuse

   This vibrant ray brings to each one all that is rightfully his own, sufficient for a given need.

7. <u>Adjustment to Life;</u> Yellow Green, Blue Green Midray

   This ray is a life regulator. The midray is self examination. This "knowing" with mental awareness and supply creates flexibility and adaptability. The attribute of adjustment to life is open-ended. It suggests a continual growth process. There is no room for rigidity and stubborn opinions here.

8. <u>Philanthropy:</u> Deep Green, Touch of Blue Underlay

    This is a strong energy ray. This color reveals generous, open-handed good will. One who gives freely needs this ray to attain balanced giving. Two spiritual rays, Love of Life and of Mankind, and Power to Control Emotion enhance this quality.

9. <u>Integrity:</u> Gray Green, Grayed Cobalt Blue Midray

    This ray symbolizes the quality of being complete, as in undivided and whole. It reveals the strength of the fiber of one's inner being. Use of this ray helps to know self, enhances basic understanding with honesty and strengthens moral courage with reliability.

10. <u>Basic Understanding:</u> Gray Green, Blue Green Midray

    This color indicates a grasp of the underlying principles of any situation whether internal or external. It gives a foundation on which to build. The midray, self-examination, helps to quicken the process.

11. <u>Generosity:</u> Gray Green with Lavender Streaks.

    This is a positive ray of giving and receiving. Its qualities extend to unselfishness, benevolence, charitability and consideration.

12. <u>Accountability:</u> Light Yellow Green, Coral Midray

    Accountability is fulfilling the responsibilities one has taken. The light yellow green of expanded awareness helps one to realize these responsibilities. The midray is the action of balanced love.

Expanded Meanings of the Psychological Rays

BLUE

Plate 3

1. <u>Evil Intent</u>: Dark Blue, Streaks of Brown and Maroon

    This reveals distortion and twisted cruelty, a plotting type of anger, calculating without mercy.

2. <u>Fear</u>: Ashen Gray Blue

    Fear is one of the deepest emotions to overcome. Its feeling is one of constriction and an inability to act naturally or freely. Sometimes fear is a good thing. It can be an instinctive drawing back from something that will give bodily harm. The color rays of Basic Understanding and Courage will help overcome Fear.

3. <u>Reliability</u>: Deep Bright Blue

    Qualities of dependability and trustworthiness vibrate within this ray. The color rays of Steadfast Confidence and Love enhance this ray.

4. <u>Emotion</u>: Deep Green Blue

    This color reminds one of the blue green of the ocean on a cloudy day. Symbolically emotion is very like the ocean, as it is a powerful force running deep and wide. Emotion in the psyche has been described as the "I, or ego, in motion". The forces of emotion push our life pattern into manisfestation. Emotion has a broad energy spectrum. It can be cold or hot, positive or negative, calm or agitated. All emotion comes from the feeling of love, and expresses according to individual experience and understanding of that truth.

5. <u>Moral Courage</u>: Bright Blue, Grayed Cobalt Blue Midray

    The side rays vibrate with the potentials of positive thinking and positive action, helping one to become conscious of one's own life standard. The midray stabilizes the life force with a calm, yet active control, integrating the outer rays.

6. <u>Justice</u>: Three Colors: Right Side, Bright Leaf Green, Left Side, Light Blue-Green; Rose Midray

    The quality of justice is right action and fair-mindedness. The leaf green at the right side reveals the attitude of open-mindedness and sound reason without bias. The midray tempers judgment with kindness. The left side of the ray is the quality of self-examination.

7. <u>Ambition:</u> Three Colors: Right Side, Cobalt Blue Lavender, Left Side, Rose Lavender with Blue, Chartreuse Midray

    This is the light ray of right ambition. The strong desire usually associated with ambition is modified by the cobalt blue, a stabilizing force. The midray attracts supply of what is rightfully one's own. The left side of the ray activates self-revelation. The full ray helps to align one with one's own reality and the purpose of one's sojourn. One can, then, aspire toward that objective. This ray is helpful in clarifying direction of purpose and in overcoming indifference and confusion.

8. <u>Loyalty:</u> Light Bright Blue

    This quality, often referred to as "true blue", is one of positive action. The conscious force within this ray stabilizes the will to fulfill any obligation. Qualities related to Loyalty are Trust, Confidence, Steadfastness and Faithfulness. The color rays of Love and Steadfast Confidence enhance the power of this ray.

9. <u>Responsibility:</u> Bright Royal Blue, Rose Midray

    This blue develops the capacity to perceive the distinctions between right and wrong. The midray of love is the developing power for this activity. The qualities related to this ray are trustworthiness, accountability, dependability and reliability. One who has this ray permanently in his aura can be counted on to fulfill a trust without encroaching on another's responsibility.

10. <u>Innate Refinement:</u> Royal Blue on the Right Side shading to Light Lavender on the Left.

    This reveals gentle kindness inherent in one's nature. Related qualities are graciousness, dignity, tact and consideration for others.

11. <u>Life's Harmony:</u> Soft Light Blue, Touch of Lavender

    This ray creates pleasing relationships in the whole of life. As a life becomes balanced one experiences the emergence of creative spiritual power and well-being. The harmony of this blue ray will do much to relieve conflict and dissension.

12. <u>Self-Analysis:</u> Light Green Blue, Light Yellow Midray

    The energy in this ray helps one to examine one's traits of disposition and character. The midray supplies the enlightenment needed.

Expanded Meanings of the Psychological Rays

YELLOW

Plate 4

1. <u>Deceit:</u> Orange streaked with Dark Brown and Dark Green

   This is a negative ray of falseness, concealment or misrepresentation. The nature of deceit is one of intense desire to cover or to hide. Deceit has its roots in fear. The color rays of Honesty and Integrity, with Love, will help to clear and transform this condition.

2. <u>Gossip:</u> Orange streaked with Henna Brown and Dark Gray Green

   This ray reveals a desire to talk idly about others, sometimes maliciously behind their backs. The colors of Moral Courage, Friendship and Life's Harmony are helpful in changing this trait.

3. <u>Cowardice:</u> Medium Yellow Gray-Green; Yellow Ochre Midray dirtied with Gray-Green

   Cowardice is a conscious restriction of the light of life, an unwillingness to participate in life for fear of being injured physically or emotionally. The restriction carried to extreme can be life-threatening. Antidotes include the colors of Heroic Courage, Moral Courage, Creative Life Force and many others.

4. <u>Scandal:</u> Strong Orange overlaid with Brown and Olive Green

   The ray of scandal is similar to the ray of gossip except that its activity is more damaging. This ray needs to be cooled by a grayed cobalt blue to help to control the emotion. Follow the blue with the rose of Love.

5. <u>Desire:</u> Strong Orange

   This is a blending of mental and emotional awareness with the Creative Life Force. Desire is the impetus which activates change, and is basic to life. Intent determines the direction of this powerful energy.

6. <u>Happiness:</u> Bright Yellow

   Happiness is the result of expressing the best that is within one. This ray brings transforming light to help overcome depression and criticism.

7. <u>Appreciation:</u> Light Pink Orange

    Awareness of the true value of what everyone has is integrated by the power of love. This combination soothes discord and dis-ease, complements positive thinking and enhances harmony in the life.

8. <u>Mental Peace:</u> Light Yellow, Coral Midray

    This may also be described as a mind at ease. The light yellow sides are very enlightening. Like the sunlight this yellow is the catalyst that lifts into light and helps to clear confusion. The midray activates awareness and stimulates clarity.

9. <u>Steadfast Confidence:</u> Yellow with Soft Brown overlay, Rich Yellow Midray

    This combination of colors gives supportive strength each to the other. Steadfast Confidence is a combination of inner strength and outer expression. Steadfastness gives balance to confidence so that it has the necessary stability.

10. <u>Motivation:</u> Rosy Copper

    This is a ray of action. Through this ray flows a combination of common sense, sunlight of happiness and power to help one follow through. This is a positive ray to overcome apathy and procrastination.

11. <u>Common Sense:</u> Salmon Pink overlaid with Burnt Sienna

    Common sense is good sense. The ray reveals sound judgment and basic intelligence. The burnt sienna gives the ray its practical quality, and the warmth of the salmon pink stimulates memory. This is an excellent ray to use when working with everyday problems.

12. <u>Intellect:</u> Rich Yellow, touch of Pale Brown, Pale Coral Midray

    Intellect is the mental power of thinking and knowing. The midray aids in balancing the physical and mental-emotional aspects of life.

Expanded Meanings of the Psychological Rays

RED

Plate 5

1. <u>Heroic Courage:</u> Bright Red

    This bright ray stimulates action which is bold and brave with fearless daring and no thought of self.

2. <u>Hatred:</u> Orange and Olive Green heavily overlaid with Intense Maroon Red

    This reveals intense dislike, animosity, enmity and loathing with strong desire to promote the little self.

3. <u>Lust:</u> Muddy Orange Green, Dirty Orange Midray

    This ray reveals an aggressive nature determined to go to any lengths to satisfy its strong appetites.

4. <u>Anger:</u> Red Orange, Bright Red Midray

    This ray reveals a strong feeling arising from displeasure, antagonism, resentment, wrath, rage or even fury. Loss of energy through anger lowers resistance to disease. The color of grayed cobalt blue is very helpful to calm this emotion.

5. <u>Greed:</u> Grayed Olive Green, Dirty Orange Midray

    This ray reveals a selfish, grasping nature with an intense desire for possessions, wealth and power. The rays of Generosity and Love will help to modify Greed.

6. <u>Creative Life Force:</u> Rich Rose Red

    Creative Life Force, like the life blood in the physical body, carries nutrients of creative energy throughout the aura, stimulating change and transformation. It helps to restore vitality.

7. <u>Love:</u> Pink Rose Lightly underlaid with Pale Orange

    The quality of love is intrinsic to all life. "Love is the great invisible pattern of God's creation, and recreation, the never-ending answer to all the question marks in man's consciousness from the simplest to the most profound." — Mary D. Weddell.

8. <u>Joy:</u> Light Salmon Pink

    The nature of joy is delight and gladness. It can become an awareness of the spiritual power within.

9. <u>Friendship:</u> Three Colors (Right to Left): Rose Pink, Orange Coral, Flesh Pink

    The basis of friendship is what each person <u>is</u>, not what either can get. This is shown in this ray by selfless love on the right, by respect and trust on the left and by mutual support in the center.

10. <u>Honor:</u> Three Colors (Right to Left): Rich Rose Lavender, Bright Yellow, Deep Lavender Rose

    The colors comprising honor may be said to represent esteem, faith and the developing action of the sun, which causes both the other qualities to grow. It develops the kind of happiness that comes from the inner knowing that one is doing what is right.

11. <u>Pride:</u> Soft Red Orange streaked with Purple

    Pride can be the result of successfully using faith to fulfill a desire. Pride is healthy when it results from competition with oneself. Self-esteem and self-respect are aspects of pride. Seen aurically the orange has a thin veiling of purple. If the colors are fused a brown purple results, indicating false pride and its unpleasant relatives such as conceit, disdain, haughtiness and arrogance.

12. <u>Aggression:</u> Three Colors (Right to Left): Rosy Salmon Pink, Sky Blue, Flesh Pink

    This color energizes one to actively use his God-given talents for good. Assertiveness in its best sense is closely related to this positive ray.

Recognition of the colors in one's psychological realm opens the door to further awareness and color expression. The Spiritual Arcs of Green, Blue, Yellow, Red and Purple (Plates 9, 10, 11, 12, 8) have to do directly with spiritual development. As has already been mentioned, many of the psychological rays touch the spiritual in vibration. The Spiritual Arcs will be discussed next.

Expanded Meanings of the Basic Spiritual Rays

ARC OF GREEN — GROWTH

Plate 9

The <u>First Ray of Green</u>, a dark green and dull grayish brown with orange at the left side, serves a very important purpose, for it is the color at the base of the aura in which each one stands. It penetrates any surface, reaching beneath the feet. Without it there is no grounding. When this ray is seen as high as the knees it indicates a sluggish, dull-blind consciousness with little interest in anything. The orange, no matter how dulled or covered over, is an expression of desire, of at least some self-assertion, an indication of potential for growth.

The <u>Second Ray of Green</u> has nearly the same colors as the first ray. The orange of desire or assertion or power of impetus upward — has moved from the left, the side of spiritual infilling, to the middle of the ray. This assertive power interacting with the dark olive green is fundamental righteousness, zealousness, self-centeredness and stubborn opinions.

The <u>Third Ray of Green</u> is a dark forest green with a blue midray. The forest green represents the earth level magnetic energy and the blue midray a spiritual force. The combination serves to give a balanced foundation to the individual life, centered and safe. Its gift is poise, stability and the quality of fair-mindedness. These important characteristics provide a base upon which to cultivate additional spiritual qualities.

The <u>Fourth Ray of Green,</u> the color of new grass, symbolizes the reality experienced in the school of life. The yellowish tone of enlightenment in the green adds an increased perception in order to understand these life realities. The hue gives energy to accept the challenges in life and move into action. This acceptance short-circuits self-deception, removes fear and resentment and opens new doors to a greater, clearer reality in a situation or attitude. The vibration of this ray works in large or small problems, in a life-threatening situation or in an irritating daily chore. It can provide enlightened energy. Acceptance of the challenge brings help from higher sources.

The <u>Fifth Ray of Green,</u> a more vivid shade of green than previous rays, is centered by an old-rose midray. The glow of the old-rose complements the vibrancy of the green, bringing in universal energy to open one to a higher consciousness. This new, more complete understanding brings into one's life an expanded perception allowing flexibility in action and attitude. Opinions of others are more easily acknowledged. The vibration of this ray awakens one into the inspired understanding of higher universal forces.

The <u>Sixth Ray of Green,</u> a beautifully clear blue-tinted emerald green, shows one who is reevaluating his life, priorities and approach to differing ideas and problems. The blue overtone in the green symbolizes the higher spiritual reality merged into the physical energy of the green. Blended, these two hues lift one's consciousness as they are absorbed and applied in daily living. This is like a rebirth, as the recognition and use of spiritual principles sustains and further develops spiritual consciousness.

The <u>Seventh Ray of Green,</u> a silvered olive green with overtones of old-rose to the left, reveals the age of the soul. This is shown by the two colors added to the olive green: the silver implies the Christ influence, and the old-rose the higher universal force mentioned earlier. The more rose, the greater the God-power being utilized in the soul.

The <u>Eighth Ray of Green,</u> two shades of moss green with a light blue midray, indicates a readiness for further development. The stabilizing energy of the green at the right is lightened through the influence of the spiritual blue midray to become a more heightened energy at the left. This ray indicates to a spiritual teacher, sensitized to understand seekers, that a hidden potential for further development can be encouraged.

The <u>Ninth Ray of Green,</u> apple green with a blue midray, gives the willing seeker what he needs in order to bring into his consciousness the aggressiveness of the little ego and its need of cleansing and direction. A person must have two outstanding qualities: (1) a willingness to see one's faults and limitations and (2) the faith to develop positive virtues. This color is tempered by the blue midray, which gives him detachment as he seeks to listen, and to modify strong opinions. This ray helps in seeking wisdom, helps to overcome faults and to bring spiritual reality into the consciousness.

The <u>Tenth Ray of Green,</u> a soft seafoam green, appropriately signifies the relentless rhythm of the great ocean tides, for this ray symbolizes the Law of Compensation, "Whatsoever a man sows, that he will also reap", what comes in must go out, where there is cause there is effect. This ray helps the seeker to be alert and receptive to the inflowing currents of soul wisdom to replace the ego-centered concepts. One who uses this ray is expanding his higher consciousness and transforming his thinking. Wider choices are now available. More of the long range consequences of his thoughts and acts can be seen. The tenth ray of green is a balancing ray which encourages growth. This growth constantly challenges one to new goals and helps one to recognize unrewarding patterns. This high level or state of balance brings freedom.

The <u>Eleventh Ray of Green,</u> a light yellow green with soft blue midray, soars higher in vibration. More yellow in the green adds enlightenment to the basic energy and the blue adds a spiritual midray. In combination, the two colors signify that one has accepted responsibility, experienced the joy of accomplishment, and a measure of peace as the vibrations of the ray enter the seeker's soul in a complete at-one-ment with Self.

The <u>Twelfth Ray of Green,</u> a delicate yellow green, at-one-ment with God, is the height of growth in the Green Arc. More and more light has been added as the soul has sought advancement. Through following a path of self-control the seeker has utilized physical energy and effort to accept challenges and refine the self with more and more spiritual light until he has grown in balance within himself. The illumination guides his steps as the seeker listens to the inner voice of the spiritual man and follows that guidance.

Expanded Meanings of the Basic Spiritual Rays

ARC OF BLUE — TRAINING OF THE EGO

Plate 10

The First Ray of Blue is very dark blue, almost black in color, with purple at the right side. The ray indicates testing that comes from the challenges of life, an awakening to a realization that there is much more to be attained and refined. The purple is the faith that is needed to accept challenges.

The first ray of blue shows one venturing into a new inner consciousness, becoming aware that life is more than merely existing. The soul senses the possibility of expanded consciousness. One is aware of having a long way to go without seeing the outcome, but has faith to take the next step.

The Second Ray of Blue is a dark blue with a stripe of bright red at the left. This ray indicates that this soul has already had repeated life experiences. The red offers the power to make conscious choices to pursue further spiritual development.

The Third Ray of Blue is a bright blue. It helps one to be aware of one's good qualities, talents and accomplishments and to have a positive outlook on life. With this color, one can take a positive stand and communicate it. There is no fear of speaking up for a cause or for oneself when one knows the source of talents. The challenge of this ray is to become aware at several levels — that besides the inflatable little self there is a knowing subconscious awareness and a higher intuitive Self through which higher power is activated.

The Fourth Ray of Blue is a light cobalt or light Wedgewood blue. The gray overtones provide the holding force of a great usable power to control emotion and to prevent waste of power. This ray enables one to begin to relate effectively to other people, to the environment as a whole and with oneself. The fourth ray neither transforms nor suppresses energy. It gives one the power to control it. In actively using the fourth ray one is acknowledging the need for this inner God-power in order to control emotion. As one begins allowing feelings and emotions to emerge and tries controlling them, progress results.

The Fifth Ray of Blue is a Copenhagen blue, a deep green-blue, an energized emotional force which activates inner feelings and sensitivities. Intuition is being awakened, often on a level of hunches. Heightened sensitivity is the key. It can manifest in the area of ego and remembrance of past hurts or focus on the needs and pains of others. One may be suddenly sensitive to the wonders of life and overwhelmed by them.

The Sixth Ray of Blue is blue touched with gray, bordered by yellow sides which support and enlighten. There is a conscious alignment with the source of power. The will is fortified and directed by the inner God-power rather than by the sensitive emotions of the personality. This ray helps to stabilize the activity of the will.

The Seventh Ray of Blue, a deep blue-green jade and gray, is a very strong energy and denotes a conscious need of victory over the little self, a great soul urge to do and to conquer. Here one needs guidance so that the energy will be well-placed and its force gentled. The inner knower realizes its need of divine alignment — connection with the universal power through the Christ within. There is more work to be done in refining, defining and balancing the emotional ego.

The Eighth Ray of Blue, with its grayed blue-green center and yellow sides, is similar in appearance to the sixth ray. However, the yellow of the eighth has more light — it is the enlightenment of the higher Self. There is no question here of will. Rather, it is a question of how one goes about it. The divine force of the eighth gentles impetuousness and impatience through spiritual growth much as a mute on a violin softens the tone of the instrument, or a transformer on a radio changes the power in the incoming wire to suit the delicate wire of the radio.

The Ninth Ray of Blue is a light turquoise. With this ray man sees his fine qualities and talents as well as his negative traits. He is able to see truth of self. With growth in understanding, confusion lessens, makin it possible for him to make spiritual decisions more easily.

The Tenth Ray of Blue, delicate opaline blue, blends the higher vibrations of love, awareness and God-power, lifted in light, to further empower spiritual balance. With the little self out of the way there is more room for the inflow of this power. Development of this ray enables one to tell the difference between messages that reveal truth and those that are of the imagination. Its use develops integration of spiritual powers. The ray helps one to interpret his dreams and visions with deeper insight thus making them more valuable to him.

The Eleventh Ray of Blue, the blue of the sky, is the ray of selfless prayer. The spiritual life is more fully lived day by day. One is less concerned with his little self and more concerned with his brother's needs.

The Twelfth Ray of Blue, light irridescent sky blue, is fourth-dimensional consciousness, that is, a realization of man as a spiritual being growing in conscious realization of the oneness of the two worlds, visible and invisible. The spiritual voice which reveals one to one's self is stronger because it is consulted more often. When touching this height one finds a blessing, a sense of comfort and companionship, a feeling of never being alone.

Expanded Meanings of the Basic Spiritual Rays

ARC OF YELLOW — ILLUMINATION

Plate 11

The First Ray of Yellow, a brown mustard color, denotes one who has strong opinions, is very set, self-asserting and dominant. The darkness of this first ray of yellow indicates a somewhat dense approach to life. What light illumines this person comes from the steadfastness of his position, which he maintains relentlessly. He has not formed the habit of listening to other opinions but continues to hold old, often outmoded ideas, simply because they are his. These ideas may reflect a strong spiritual intolerance. The strong opinions and self-assertiveness may convey strength to a student, and thus such a person makes a good teacher.

The Second Ray of Yellow, golden ochre with a bit of flame in it, carries forward the dominance of the first ray. The second ray indicates a person who has had numerous earth lives, many experiences and testings but has not learned from them. In some matters, this person thinks he knows all there is to know and is extremely sensitive to criticism. He does not want to hear the facts or start thinking in a different way.

The Third Ray of Yellow is a chartreuse green with an overlay of buff. The buff is a carryover of stubbornness from the second ray. It represents a clinging to possessions, an unwillingness to share knowledge. When the buff is cleared from this ray, the spiritual greed disappears and we have a ray of giving and taking and of supply of all good. One has outgrown the ray's limitations and is now ready to receive yet more light.

The Fourth Ray of Yellow, a canary yellow, is a vigorous, active spiritual energy. This ray indicates a choice made — to identify one's life consciously with spiritual principles and to earnestly try to stay integrated by spirit. The inflow of spiritual light available with this ray feeds one's inner being. Intuition increases and mental processes are sharpened.

The Fifth Ray of Yellow is a five-part ray. It is a ray of introspection, one of self-testing and recognition of growth attempted and growth achieved.

The pink orchid reveals that man is on a quest of spirit. Because it has purple in it, the color provides a measure of balance and staying power.

The deep rose is asking forgiveness. This can be accomplished only through Love, and the deep rose is the color of Christ Love.

The pale yellow shows rebirth into greater enlightenment. All the soul searching and work done in the forgiving process has made this new light possible.

The tangerine represents man's habits of the past. This color gives a strong spiritual desire to search out and overcome those things which might slow his progress toward enlightenment. The strong vibratory activity of the tangerine along with the pale yellow will help to identify and to cleanse the unwanted traits.

The fifth color is brown, symbolizing the rugged earthly path man must travel. The little, personal self is what he must overcome, and in the overcoming there is freedom.

The Sixth Ray of Yellow is often called the "Silver Cord". This radiant ray appears to be very pale blue with an underlay of yellow. The silver cord is referred to in the Scriptures (Eccl. 12:6) and has been known to exist from time immemorial. It is like an etheric counterpart of the physical umbilical cord and as such is the lifeline that guides the soul's return back to the physical body. It is attenuated when one is out of the body, stretching as far as needed, and is severed only at death.

The <u>Seventh Ray of Yellow</u> is composed of four colors — yellow orange, rose, pastel rose and pale yellow. This ray reveals the source of supply to the aura. It is the radiant energy flowing from the God-center of life. As the God-life consciousness matures, the color of the orb floating within this ray deepens in richness, from pale yellow of less enlightenment to the sun yellow of more enlightenment. The ray supplies light or illumination to the aura, and its location indicates the degree of development attained.

The <u>Eighth Ray of Yellow,</u> peach pink, truly reflects the glow of a warm affectionate person. Because of his kindly, approachable nature he is willing to help others, often suppressing his own desires and needs in order to do so. He recognizes his need for spiritual guidance from within and from without, eagerly anticipating an earthly teacher to lead him to his spiritual goals. He might do well to trust the old adage, "When the student is ready the teacher will appear."

The <u>Ninth Ray of Yellow</u> is an apricot pink, one of the colors of balance. It contains a lofty spiritual desire and much inner light and merges the qualities of appreciation and enlightened love. These colors also reveal a soul who is alert to great contrasts in the life about him — of joy and sorrow, happiness and suffering. Eager and balanced, he, too, is ready for a teacher to lead him to higher development. He loves wisely, so he is tolerant of mankind and knows that love is the remedy for all things.

The <u>Tenth Ray of Yellow</u> is deep rose to flesh. This ray shows one whose love nature is intensified, made possible by the release from the subconscious of significant amounts of energy formerly used in maintaining old habits and modes of thinking. That released energy has been transformed by love to increased loving capacity. Because he has been infilled with a Love tempered by Spirit, all his expressions of love are appropriate, timely, with no excesses. This person knows himself thoroughly and has learned to judge himself truly. He can therefore judge others without prejudice. He can see clearly and evaluate truly. He does not criticize. He respects himself and all men. (The color of Respect is the flesh color at the left side of the ray.)

The <u>Eleventh Ray of Yellow</u>, a rich sun yellow, describes the maturing process. It is a ray of developing action, feeding and stimulating spiritual growth. A person radiating this color sees the picture all around and in depth because his vision is expanded by Spirit. He has grown through much searching giving him a deep understanding of another's search.

Just as the sun makes chemical changes in green fruit, bringing it to sweet ripeness, so the rich spiritual sun yellow makes chemical changes in man's nature. It "ripens" his good traits and gives him a new sweetness of character. Spiritual expression toward his fellow man then comes easily. The separated has become integrated. He now sees and understands the great pattern of life alive within his God-center, his Christ Consciousness, and thus is able to fit into this great pattern. He now truly can bring spiritual expression into daily living. He can see his earth life in terms of spiritual lessons. Happiness has matured into joy in the soul.

The <u>Twelfth Ray of Yellow</u> is a beautiful sunset color, flame pink to yellow. It is a God Ray of a developed person, many times seen and described as gold about a person. This is the ray that the Renaissance artists depicted in many of their paintings as a golden circle about the head or a radiating nimbus surrounding the person.

Expanded Meanings of the Basic Spiritual Rays

ARC OF RED — METAMORPHOSIS

Plate 12

The <u>First Ray of Red</u> has a light orange-yellow center with rose-orange at each side. This color combination indicates one is on the very brink of discovering the potential spiritual power latent within each soul. This potential power, as in any other latent seed energy, shows a power that is a possibility. Results are imaginable — not actually fulfilled but expectable, probable. Its power will grow with faithful use. Realizing the transforming power of the ray can release that ray for overcoming. As the seeker is presented with numerous opportunities in daily life to test this faith, the energy of the ray becomes a clearing, cleansing force.

The <u>Second Ray of Red</u> has streaks of brilliant red and orange. It holds anger and its derivatives such as quick anger, pride of opinion, self-glorification, exaggeration and criticism. These cripple new growth. Often an angry outburst is triggered by falling short of one's own expectations. It boomerangs, giving one a sickening feeling at the solar plexus. Following a personal setback, forgiveness, forbearance, patience, prayer and control of emotion are some of the remedies.

Pride of opinion is so difficult to recognize, so easy to justify that one is not aware of its subtle influence on self and others. The difference between having a right to an opinion and its outbreak in uncontrol needs to be discerned. Self-glorification, the sudden push of the self, claiming either superiority or inferiority, can be indicated by this color.

Exaggeration can be a harmless means of making a story more interesting. Yet it often can muddy the purpose of whatever is being attempted. However, the purpose in spiritual pursuits is to seek Truth, which never needs embellishment, only discernment.

Criticism of self or others blocks further development. The Color plume for overcoming a critical nature is shown in this volume. (See Plate 6).

The <u>Third Ray of Red,</u> soft red, green and yellow, is life force expressed by spirit. This is a spiritual ideal where man's physical mental-emotional and spiritual bodies work together to blend into an harmonious whole. At the universal level, it would indicate all nations of men unified and cooperating. The colors are soft: red the physical body, green the mental-emotional body and yellow the spiritual body. Pigments rarely catch the essence of the Third Ray of Red. Layers of fine silk chiffon in soft rose, green and yellow, constantly moving against sparkles of light can give some idea of the true appearance of this important balancing ray.

This Third Ray is of very high quality. It creates a higher degree of balance than has previously been achieved. One with this ray speaks the truth without exaggeration. The Third Ray of Red has been called the core of spiritual growth. Much loving watchfulness and conscious effort are required to maintain it.

The <u>Fourth Ray of Red</u>, red, purple, maroon, yellow, marks a definite stage in metamorphosis. Just as the adult butterfly's egg hatches a larva which spins a cocoon and emerges as a winged, airy creature of irridescent beauty and a wondrous internal guidance system, so man. Man is on his way to becoming a spiritual being with an aura of luminous beauty, aware of his sonship, and capable of living joyously in eternity now. A person displaying the Fourth of Red in his aura has proven his faith sufficiently and achieved enough balance to enable him to handle the increased power contained in the ray.

The colors are a specific arrangement of red, purple, maroon and yellow stripes, indicating higher forces entering the spiritual path. They show one on the path of the Christ, willing to lay down the "old man", ready for the "new man", born anew. The path is an Inner Channel, a oneness with the God-center within. One makes this path his own by living the Christ principles in day to day living as demonstrated by Jesus. One is born into the physical life with the eternal life breathed into him. Here, in the earth school, one is given the opportunity to develop the Christ Consciousness of the spiritual life. Through the growth and development of this training, one is indeed born again into his spiritual being — the new man, in touch with the treasure within. When one expresses a willingness to lay aside the "old man" — old habits and faults — the Fourth Ray of Red gives a powerful message to one's subconscious. A new life is made. He is aware of his oneness — a spiritual being within a physical body. New challenges are overcome because there is a willingness to change.

The <u>Fifth Ray of Red</u> has deep red on the right, a brown streak in the middle and rose red on the left. The deep red signifies the awareness that there is a need to struggle with one's worldly self and to overcome its negative traits. It involves looking at that which one would rather keep hidden but must see in order to meet the test of this ray. Here, as truth of self is revealed and examined, man desires to do something about it. As a result, a deep cleansing takes place, often a painful process of going within to face old habitual faults together with the emotions and attitudes attached to them. Learning of the Christ Way — the way of Love — leads to victory.

The dried blood color in the center, activator of the struggle, does not allow one to stand still, only to go forward or back. By asking forgiveness and laying aside the old as a sacrifice of self, one bridges the hard-won revelation of the deep red with the victory of the rose red at the left. One has a choice of abandoning the revealed faults all at once or dealing with each inner revelation separately. Whichever the choice, one acknowledges the supremacy of the inner man over the outer man.

One of the meanings of the Fifth Ray of Red is the biblical struggle of forty days in the wilderness which can be interpreted literally or symbolically. Many religions and cultures embrace this symbolism by various methods of cleansing and self-examination. Forty days, either intermittent or consecutive, seem to be sufficient to cleanse and renew. In Creative Color this inner viewing is meant to be a deeply loving, compassionate process in which understanding, forgiveness and love are of greatest importance. To hasten this healing, one can demand of the subconscious that all energy from the old faults be transmuted into usable, creative energy. The victory represented by the rose red at the left symbolizes this process of transmutation.

The <u>Sixth Ray of Red,</u> a beautifully quiet ray of rose red on the right merging into coral pink on the left, is the ray of clear thinking and pure purpose, the emergence of wisdom, promising spiritual sight and comprehension of dreams and visions.

This ray assists one in assimilating the import of the two previous rays for it helps to discriminate between the good and the less good. The color of this ray can assist at any time in defining goals and determining priorities in keeping with one's spiritual unfoldment. It brings thoughts to a focal point and helps one to verbalize them. After distilling personal experiences and extracting truth from them, one finds his purpose clear.

The Seventh Ray of Red, salmon pink with a wide midray of cerise, means a soul seeking, with great power for development and the perseverance needed to do so. There is also a desire to share the treasures of the inner life one has discovered.

The Eighth Ray of Red, plum, red and yellow stripes, shows one on the path of Christ Consciousness. This person is determined to follow the spiritual way. He has balanced enthusiasm, his energy is directed Godward. He carries his load willingly, happy and content. This ray could denote a consistently even-tempered person. The steady seeking growth of the Eighth Ray of Red brings happiness and contentment. One with this ray would gladly help all those who asked. He would share his happiness and give assurance or a fresh point of view, and a visitor would never go away empty-handed or discouraged.

The Ninth Ray of Red consists of alternating stripes of light blue and light rose. It denotes one who is demonstrating selflessness and who has overcome bigotry. It shows one who is living a Christ-centered life, using the proper level of vibration suitable to the task or occupation. Such a person would be consciously and habitually living in a high spiritual consciousness.

The Tenth Ray of Red, coral rose with a flesh pink center, shows a nature resplendent in warmth and the virtues of kindness. This person is considerate and thoughtful of others' needs and has a talent for making the best of things. This talent includes transcending tragedy, bringing out the best in people, changing the direction of a potentially quarrelsome conversation, making a special occasion of a simple meal through the addition of love, being open to intuitive guidance and to creative solutions to difficult situations.

The Eleventh Ray of Red appears as a light pink, at times seen with an inner glow of yellow bisque. This ray means tenderness and concern for a brother. Here is the triumph of selflessness, putting others first, no desire for praise. The Eleventh of Red puts humanitarian principles into direct action, sometimes on a grand scale, often on a one-to-one basis. Though one with this ray prominent in his aura often steps in the shade to allow another to come forward, he does not shirk his responsibilities but takes the lead when guided to do so. The qualities of the Eleventh Ray include wisdom, strength, humility and kindly, selfless thoughtfulness of others.

The Twelfth Ray of Red, soft grayed old rose, indicates a universal concept of life, tolerance with understanding. Tolerance is necessary to the success of rays Seven through Eleven, but tolerance accompanied by full understanding comes with this Twelfth Ray. The Twelfth of Red, like others of the Spiritual Red rays, helps us to attain lasting changes in soul development. Here, there enters into the life a rich appreciation of inner and outer realities, an inner transcending that reaches out in wordless praise. Here, one grows in ability to sense and then to realize many degrees of vibration. With this maturing sensitivity one feels and knows that God is everywhere and within all that is, comforting and blessing us with this delicate color.

Color Descriptions and Meanings

BASIC SPIRITUAL ARC OF PURPLE — SPIRITUAL BALANCE

Plate 8

1st Ray: <u>Four Stripes (Right to Left): Soft Gray, Soft Gray Lavender, Rose Pink and Blue Lavender</u>

    Meaning: Soft Gray .... Yearning
               Soft Gray Lavender .... Longing
               Rose Pink .... Aspiration
               Blue Lavender .... Self Revelation

2nd Ray: <u>Royal Purple</u>

    Meaning: Faith

3rd Ray: <u>Blue Plum</u>

    Meaning: Depth of Love

4th Ray: <u>Rose Purple</u>

    Meaning: Divine Imagination

5th Ray: <u>Red Plum</u>

    Meaning: Spiritual Wisdom

6th Ray: <u>Soft Rose Lilac</u>

    Meaning: Charity

7th Ray: <u>Brilliant Rose Fuschia</u>

    Meaning: Sympathetic Understanding

8th Ray: <u>Grayed Pink Lavender</u>

    Meaning: Harmony

9th Ray: <u>Rose Peach</u>

    Meaning: Gratitude

10th Ray: <u>Light Blue Lavender</u>

    Meaning: Peace

11th Ray: <u>Rose Bisque</u>

    Meaning: Grace

12th Ray: <u>Blush Orchid</u>

    Meaning: Serenity

Expanded Meanings of the Basic Spiritual Rays

ARC OF PURPLE — SPIRITUAL BALANCE

Plate 8

Together, the twelve Basic Rays of the Arc of Purple denote spiritual balance. The purple rays, more than those of other arcs, are in two parts: one through six personal, seven through twelve universal. These rays denote personal commitment to and responsibility for that portion of interaction and leadership demanded by one's destiny.

The qualities which the rays of the Arc of Purple represent have inspired many spiritual writings. Every quality is available to man when recognized, accepted, appreciated and put to use. All can be earned. None can be purchased or bartered. Once attained they cannot be sold and they wither with disuse. As one grows with the qualities, one increasingly savors the joy of living in the rhythm, emerging more and more from one's center, in peace and with minimal stress. The path upward is traveled in joyous harmony with all life.

Purple is the predominant color in the arc but not the only one. Gratitude and Grace have no purple in them but they are often seen with a lavender overglow, and they are essential to the balancing process. A person whose spiritual development is proceeding in a balanced manner will have one or more of the purple rays in his aura, showing development to a degree compatible with his growth in the other arcs.

The First Ray of Purple consists of a group of four interacting colors. They are listed in the order of their four progressive meanings, right to left: Yearning, soft gray, Longing, soft gray lavender, Aspiration, rose pink, and Self-revelation, blue lavender.

The Yearning of the First Ray of Purple shows conscious, intense eagerness to go as high as possible, to be and to live as God intended, to live up to one's highest potential. Longing is even more intense, the longing perhaps to touch the vibration of the Master Jesus, to be open to the leading of the higher Self. Yearning to go beyond the known and the intense longing for union with one's own God-center are a type of homesickness, longing for one's spiritual home.

No amount of wishing, thinking, pondering or even yearning and longing will produce progress until that feeling is given direction. The rose pink of Aspiration gives that direction — upward, outward, onward. Aspiration lifts one above the vague longings into the realm of possibilities for it has the power to give vitality to other qualities. From this elevation beautiful writings can come, sometimes a song of the soul. There may be a sense here of entering new territory, beginning new adventures, of daring to become all one can be. Just "being" is not enough at this point.

The rose pink of Aspiration is a delicate but strong, high form of love. It can be, literally, breathing the air of a higher level, love of the spirit. It is a high vibration. To realize this ray one must step out of the material and consciously aspire to the radiance of lighted love.

The color of <u>Self-Revelation,</u> a blue lavender, will help one to glimpse not only the great positive possibilities but also will reveal traits which need correction so that the goal may be achieved with more ease and less struggle. Thus, the First Ray of Purple is the entrée to the world of spiritual balance and is necessary to achieve the next step higher.

The <u>Second Ray of Purple</u>, the royal purple of Faith, is the essential ingredient in any spiritual activity. Faith engages the intellect in order to bypass it. Faith is used in some form daily by every human soul. Faith contributes to many other qualities in the various color arcs but they do not directly derive from it. Faith simply is. Its position at the base of the Inner Channel is significant. The rich, high vibration of the royal purple enlivens all of man's attributes.

The <u>Third Ray of Purple,</u> Depth of Love, blue plum in color, encompasses and goes far beyond human love. It is both impersonal and deeply personal, with no trace of selfishness, totally unconditional. It includes love of one's children and of one's artistic creations, love of gifts received from God and awareness of being a channel for those gifts. At its highest level, it denotes the deepest love of God's reflection in the self and acceptance of that at-one-ment. Through this ray, one touches the fundamental motivation for being in this life. The silvery film, or "bloom", is the touch of the Christ Spirit.

The <u>Fourth Ray of Purple,</u> the rose amethyst of Divine Imagination, is the open door to higher consciousness. One learns to distinguish between psychological imagery and spiritual imagery or divine imagination. Both are needed. Man's ability to envision a possible occurrence, to hear inwardly, to close his eyes and journey in imagination to far places, to "see" a stage drama while reading a play or a book is a great gift. Fantasy and daydreaming are also forms of imagination. All of these lie in the realm of psychological imagery. This ability to create mental pictures is related to the ability to receive visual impressions from the higher realms, to have visions and to recall dreams. Those persons who claim to have no ability to receive mental pictures may have blocked the ability. They may be expecting too much — pictures clear as photographs, for instance. They may be skilled in some other form of communication such as directed writing. The color of Divine Imagination can assist one in developing and balancing whatever talent one has along this line.

The <u>Fifth Ray of Purple</u>, the red plum of Spiritual Wisdom, has a rose orange underglow which combines desire with love and lifts it to a higher plane. It contains, as well, the colors of Faith, Love and Peace at the Earth Level. Here is timeless wisdom intelligently applied. It is the wisdom one expects to hear from a great spiritual teacher. It comes from a great height and therefore has an elevated perspective on all factors involved in any problem. It suggests good solutions to benefit all concerned.

The <u>Sixth Ray of Purple,</u> Charity, is soft rose lilac in color. The word charity is a derivative of the Latin "caritas", meaning dear, caring, valued. Charity includes caring for and about one's own God-center as well as that of every other person's, caring enough to serve others when led to do so. Charity includes caring about as well as caring for and taking care in speaking and in thinking. It is exquisitely loving, discriminating in the best sense of the word. Charity is caring enough to use whatever time and spiritual power are necessary to carefully and prayerfully select colors for a plume. Charity is also giving another the benefit of any doubt and allowing another to have the last word.

The Seventh Ray of Purple is a brilliant rose fuschia. Its meaning, Sympathetic Understanding, is closely related to compassion. There is love in this activating color as well as clear thinking, faith, intelligence and deep feeling. Sympathetic understanding involves heart and mind working together to offer uplift to another who is distressed. This is the sympathy which shares and helps by listening, caring, silently praying, but not by joining in the grief or by taking on the pain.

The Eighth Ray of Purple, Harmony, is a soft grayed pink lavender. The colors in Harmony are from all the preceding purple rays. The stabilizing force of the gray, the controlling vibration of the blue and the warming energy of the pink merge to provide harmony. A mixture of thoughts and words, when put together it is a holding force. Harmony is a wholeness of many parts. Harmony gives the power to be in rhythm where you are, being in the love rhythm of the universe.

Harmony alone does not assure balance. For example, an entrire orchestra could be playing correctly, in tune, each section harmonious within itself, but one section might be playing so exuberantly that another section could not be heard. Balance would require a consideration of the strengths of the instruments as well as of the skillful, correct rendition of the music.

The Ninth Ray of Purple is the rose peach of Gratitude. Gratitude is always an acceptable gift to offer. It is more than thankfulness or appreciation. Gratitude is a very rich, heartfelt, overflowing appreciation.

The Tenth Ray of Purple, Peace, is a light blue lavender. The peace of the Purple Arc is of the spirit. It is neither a sleep nor a forgetting. This is the peace of perfect balance — the true repose of the human spirit. It involves a letting go, a detachment from the feelings and thoughts of the material world. It is the feeling of being in touch with heaven and earth together as if suspended between the two.

The Eleventh Ray of Purple, Grace, a rose bisque, is the strength of gentleness, the quiet unobtrusive love of God in action. It has been called the perfume of God's love. Grace is giving — in delicate, tender strength. It is the retiring of the ego that the power of spirit may manifest.

The Twelfth Ray of Purple, Serenity, is a blush orchid. Serenity is the fruit of spiritual control, the absence of the personal ego. It helps keep the three bodies — physical, mental-emotional and spiritual — in balance as the consciousness rises. The change in consciousness is similar to the physical change one experiences in climbing high mountains where oxygen may be needed. Serenity is an inward knowing and enjoyment of God's love, conscious of earth problems but consciously living above the strife.

THE BALANCING FORCE OF THE PURPLE RAYS

The developmental sequence of the five arcs of Color rays culminates in the Purple Arc of Spiritual Balance. All of the prior four Color arcs have been necessary to achieve spiritual balance. Thus, the seeker looks back on Growth, the Training of the Ego, Illumination and Metamorphosis as necessary steps to Spiritual Balance.

However, Mary often said to her students that the Purple Arc might well be placed in the middle of the other four arcs and, indeed, she had at times taught it so for it is the balancing force to the developmental sequence. Therefore, let us think about the purple rays as the maturing fulcrum for the developmental characteristics of the other four arcs. The supportive characteristics of the balancing purple rays are helpful to their numerical counterparts in other arcs. These will be further discussed in an analysis of the relationships of the basic spiritual rays to each other.

The First Ray of Purple — The yearning, longing, aspiration and self-revelation of the first ray of Purple can stimulate in a motivational manner the first rays of green, blue, yellow and red. It can help move the sluggish indifference and disinterest in growth of the first of Green, boosting the ray and helping to clear the not-very-clear orange of desire. The aspiration in the ray assists the needed refinement of the first ray of Blue by enhancing the faith in that ray. The strong opinions of the first of Yellow can be modified by the self-revelation of this first ray of Purple. And, the testing ground of Faith in the first of Red is obviously helped by all characteristics of this purple ray — yearning, longing, aspiration and self-revelation.

The Second Ray of Purple — Faith acts like a universal energizer to help the second rays of each arc. It softens the self-centeredness and stubborn opinions of the second of Green, encourages the old soul of the second of Blue who is capable of spiritual comprehension to move toward that goal, and modifies the old soul of the second of Yellow who is overconfident and loathes to be corrected. Faith in his ability to overcome would help the second of Red conquer his quick anger and self-glorification. It is indeed a "multivitamin" to all the second rays — helping the spiritual body to achieve and maintain optimum health.

The Third Ray of Purple — Depth of Love, which is perfect Love, goes deeply into the nature, enlivening the subconscious depths and rising to the height of the consciousness. It helps dissolve fears, which inhibit love. It enables more of God's love to enter the aura and thus helps increase self-esteem. Depth of Love has an especial affinity with the third rays. Depth of Love enhances the foundational balance of the third ray of Green and the active realization of good of the third of Blue. It overcomes the imbalanced accumulation characteristics of the third of Yellow and adds cohesiveness to the merging of the three bodies of the third of Red, thus establishing a balanced truth. It is a ray providing stable, steadying growth for all third level rays.

The Fourth Ray of Purple — Divine Imagination, mental imagery lifted to a spiritual level, offers inner glimpses or feelings of what awaits man when the challenges of the fourth rays are overcome. It is a motivator toward action and can help define attainable goals. It is useful in accepting the daily challenges life presents to the fourth of Green. It adds stability to the power to control emotions of the fourth of Blue. Likewise it can be a balancing aid to the person with the fourth ray of Yellow who is endeavoring to keep integrated by spirit. It gives impetus to the twice-born fourth ray of Red person who has laid down his old, outworn traits and ideas and is ready for the new. Since each of the fours contains a particularized self-discipline it is encouraging to have an idea of why such discipline is worthwhile, and Divine Imagination shows man where he can be along the path.

The Fifth Ray of Purple — Spiritual Wisdom can be an invaluable fulcrum point to all fifth rays. In the Fifth of Green the guidance of Spiritual Wisdom is needed to maintain balance while practicing flexibility and open-mindedness and in entering higher consciousness. He may choose — aided by Spiritual Wisdom — to climb the Channel more often because he needs its protection. In Blue, Spiritual Wisdom halts the unreasoned flow of emotion. In Yellow, Spiritual Wisdom helps by enlivening the memory of previous lessons. These recollections help in making decisions along the path. Spiritual Wisdom helps the Fifth of Red to choose to undergo the examination of self, the cleansing and testing of the ray as a healthy means of growth in love.

The Sixth of Purple — Charity, a love beyond emotion, would seem of basic significance for the Sixth of Green's spiritual life present in the physical and for the Sixth of Blue's will-to-do and life force stabilized. This loving force helps stabilize and protect the attenuation of the Silver Cord, the Sixth of Yellow, when one visits the higher heavens. Incorporating pure love into the Sixth of Red increases the viability of that ray's pure purpose, clear thinking and emerging wisdom.

The Seventh Ray of Purple — Sympathetic Understanding at the level of the seventh rays tends to add forgiveness and understanding of self or others. In the Seventh of Green it encourages the rose quality of the ray, giving that loving understanding and forgiveness to assist the soul's further progress. It would support the great soul urge of the Seventh of Blue. In the Seventh of Yellow, Sympathetic Understanding awakens one's understanding of the illumination received. It is supportive of the Seventh of Red, giving help and understanding of the urge to share and the need for perseverance in the spiritual quest. It makes an easy bridge between oneself and others when sharing and gives insight to a teacher.

The Eighth Ray of Purple — Harmony is an essential ingredient in any progress. In the Eighth of Green it would be choreographing the hidden development to find expression. In the Eighth of Blue it would be assisting the divine force in beautifying and modifying the ego, softening its power. For the Eighth of Yellow, Harmony would contribute a balance to one who is often too kindly and self-sacrificing. And, in the Eighth of Red, Harmony would be of assistance in directing energy Godward. Harmony will keep him on the Path. Harmony helps to integrate new growth with that already attained.

The Ninth Ray of Purple — Gratitude encourages and feeds the idealistic qualities to be found in each of the ninth Rays. Gratitude tends to soften and modify the immature and strong opinions of the Ninth of Green.

It can help the Ninth of Blue realize growth and greater self-understanding thus leading to less confusion in the life. Gratitude for the progress brings glimpses of further attainment. The Ninth of Yellow, filled with love of life and of mankind, would recognize the source of this love — God-power — and blend Gratitude with the fulfillment and use of this love. Gratitude would feed spiritual power to the Ninth of Red, selflessly developing a Christ-centered life. Expressing Gratitude habitually assures all the Rays of a continuous supply of spiritual energy.

The Tenth Ray of Purple — Peace, a powerful, active centeredness, is supportive of all spiritual qualities. Naturally attuned to the tenth spiritual rays, it helps to steady and conserve their lively, expanding, self-realizing energies. For the Tenth of Green, Peace steadies and gives strength to awareness of the Law of Compensation and the expanding consciousness. In the Tenth of Blue, Peace is needed to steady the delicacy of the qualities of 'Spiritual sight and hearing,' and being at Peace assists in discerning the difference between imagination and revelation of truth. Peace brings quietude and a steadying balance to one who is temperate in all things and walks the way of love — the Tenth of Yellow. To the Tenth of Red, kind, thoughtful of others, talented in making the best of things, Peace offers continued replenishment and a welcome refreshment in God-power.

The Eleventh Ray of Purple — Grace. All of the elevens need Grace to maintain their high spiritual state. The Eleventh of Green embodies the realization that "Not by myself but of Thee, O God, through Thy Grace do I have a measure of peace, joy in accomplishment, and do I take responsibility and feel at one with myself." In the Eleventh of Blue, Grace is needed for living the spiritual life, for selfless prayers and for reading auras, where even at this level the personality may have a tendency to impose a preconceived notion. Grace adds the needed impersonality.

Grace helps the Eleventh of Yellow keep in balance and stay on the chosen path, widening the experience of the worlds of men and ideas. The nebulous ideas obtained from exploring many paths have become synchronized into a force unifying one with the Christ Consciousness within. Constantly maturing, the individual respects and understands men of many faiths, becoming more and more spiritual in expression toward all fellowmen. Grace gives this expression the gentle finesse of the illumined diplomat. Grace energizes the tenderness and concern of the Eleventh of Red, and helps keep the tenderness intact no matter what the circumstances by holding one centered and in balance. The height of this red ray exemplifies the love described in 1 Corinthians 13, which is possible only through the Grace of God.

The Twelfth Ray of Purple, Serenity, eases the ascent to the other twelves, all of which are very high in vibration. Serenity gives each twelfth ray an opportunity to review life calmly, from a height, to gain new perspectives on life. The poise and balance of Serenity are particularly needed by the Twelfth of Green where the path is made clear through self-control, the illumination and the resultant living in at-one-ment with God. The interweaving of the colors of blush orchid and very light yellow-green gives the Twelfth of Green a light, high feeling of wholeness. Serenity steadies the realization of the fourth-dimensional consciousness in the Twelfth of Blue, enabling one to function in the dimensions of higher consciousness. Serenity can neutralize any nervous tension the Twelfth of Blue may have on becoming aware of the fourth dimension. As the consciousness recognizes and accepts the oneness of the visible and invisible worlds, Serenity gives needed poise to the receiving of the inspired word. Serenity not only steadies the bodies, it helps one assimilate the idea and the consciousness of this oneness.

The Twelfth of Yellow, God-ray of a developed person, often described as gold about a person, is at its height, a cosmic consciousness. Few experience more than brief moments of that full awareness. Serenity can give sustaining power for and a gentle return to earth-level consciousness after a special experience of illumination. Serenity's blush orchid, delicately interwoven with the soft grayed old rose of the Twelfth of Red, can balance and energize the Twelfth of Red to complete transformational changes to higher levels.

Now that you have seen how the ray qualities of one Arc can blend, strengthen and replenish other rays, you are ready to analyze how ALL of the rays can be used in varying ways — individually and supportively — to enhance other colors. The next section will help you with this, for the harmonics of the rays within the same arc and across the spectrum of an identically numbered ray in another arc, often producing chords of color, will begin to weave a tapestry of great beauty and significance to enrich your lives.

Mary Weddell offers this comment on the core of color knowledge, "Analyze and study these, make them your own and use them to comfort and heal and bless all who seek your uplifting help."

ANALYSIS OF THE RELATIONSHIPS OF THE BASIC SPIRITUAL RAYS

Albert Einstein theorized that everything in the universe has a relationship to every other thing. This is true of the color rays described in this book. Nothing is without relationship, since "everything in creation is ensouled by a tiny particle of God's intelligence".[6]

The rates of vibration or frequencies of the rays have harmonic or disharmonic relationships to each other, just as musical notes have a relationship to each other, whether harmonic or dissonant. With this thought in mind, the rays of the Spiritual Arcs of Green, Blue, Yellow and Red can be analyzed and compared. (Refer to an earlier portion of this chapter for the original definitions and their expanded meanings.)

Consider, then, self-assertion, represented by the orange at the left in the first ray of the Green Arc and also denoted in the first ray of the Yellow Arc. When seen in its proper position in the aura, at the base of the aura, the self-assertion of the green ray is expressed on the physical level. There, it is appropriately related to self-preservation, to the desire for survival. In the yellow ray, it has moved to expression on a psychological level. Opinions are strong. These opinions, manifesting psychologically, may concern spiritual matters, reflecting an aggressive spiritual intolerance. Individuals with strong opinions make good teachers because their strong opinions and self-assertiveness convey self-confidence to the student, promoting interest in the subject matter being taught. If their spiritual intolerance is modified by the potential power, the realization and overcoming of the first ray of the Red Arc, they can become truly good teachers. Otherwise, their prejudices will be passed on to their students.

Because the Red ray contains potential power, realization and overcoming, it can help to influence the person to realize the necessity to change the negative habit patterns reflected in the Yellow. He may begin to question opinions long held, though only the <u>potential</u> for change may be explored.

It is not until the third ray of the Red Arc begins to show in the aura that evidence of actual change is seen. This ray indicates that the life force is expressed by spirit: body, mind and spirit are beginning an alignment towards balance. This spiritual expression is further evidenced in the fourth ray of Yellow. With development of this ray, the individual has been endeavoring to keep the growing integration more constant, trying earnestly to express spiritual principles in his daily living. With these changes taking place, the aura would have begun to display the foundational balance of the third ray of Green.

This ray reflects a growth from the narrowness of the opinionated lower rays to a more fair-minded attitude toward all aspects of life. The dark green of energetic growth is inlaid with a shaft of blue. This Wedgewood blue holds within it the power to control emotion so that the energy is in balanced flow. The ray represents a new beginning in perspective and in investigating the meaning of life. It helps to overcome intolerance, fundamental righteousness and stubborn opinions by allowing others the right to their own (other) beliefs. When yoked with the fifth ray of Green, an open-minded curiosity towards the meaning of life results.

The fulfillment of integration and balance can be found in the Purple Arc of Spiritual Balance. However, there is much to be accomplished before all the rays of the Purple Arc are radiantly aglow in the aura.

When realization and overcoming have washed away the fierceness of inappropriately placed self-assertion and the powerful dominance of strong, set opinions, the third ray of Blue might be found showing in the aura. A more positive, less cynical outlook on life, resulting from a realization of the good in life, would begin to be a keynote of the life. The rerouting of the individual from self interest to soul interest has begun.

We might assume that the strong, stubborn opinions and fundamental righteousness of these slower vibrating rays were at last conquered by foundational balance and fairmindedness, the influence of spirit, a positive outlook and a conscious identification with spirit. But, alas, the tests are repeated again and again on higher spirals as we climb the stairway of spiritual development. The ninth ray of Green, helpful in identifying faults, still displays immaturity, though we are acutely conscious of it. And yet an individual whose aura contains this ray clings to strong mental and spiritual opinions. The ray brings to the consciousness of the seeker the aggressiveness of the little ego, the need to overcome it and to modify the strong opinions, to listen and to seek out the wisdom to overcome, and to bring spiritual reality into the consciousness.

When life's challenges are recognized and accepted, we have formed a picture of the reality of life. We don't blame others. The fear that we expressed as intolerance, insecurity and self-righteousnes in the lower Yellow rays, and the quick anger of the second ray of Red are removed by the fourth ray of Green. It suggests adaptability and flexibility which flowers in the fifth ray of the Green Arc. Whenever we accept a challenge self-confidence grows, a certainty grows within. This develops into the faith in oneself and in God of the second ray of Purple. This faith often blossoms much later into the peach pink of the eighth ray of Yellow — a willingness to follow the Leader within, and later as respect for self and all men, that is, faith in self and in others. Faith's full maturity is expressed in the twelfth rays of Green, Blue, Yellow and Red when all is given over to the God-power within.

The fourth ray of the Blue Arc brings this God-power to bear on the emotional nature — so strongly, often violently, expressed. Many of the traits symbolized by the Psychological Rays, already discussed in another part of this book, can be subdued, then conquered by the power of this ray. One must not be at the mercy of the emotions if one is to work through the tests upcoming, where the personality is bared, naked to the intent of the higher Self and, thus, where one must take a long, hard look at one's own life expression. Fortunately, some preparation has been made through the acceptance of life's challenges of the fourth ray of Green and help is ever available with the realizations encouraged by the third ray of Blue. So, even at this stage we come to know that we are not alone and that the victory of the Christ within is assured if we pursue the Path intently.

Mary Weddell often spoke of the stumbling blocks on the path of development which she called the "Lions on the Path". The fifth rays of Yellow and of Red, wherein we view these "lions" in a comprehensive way, are assisted by the insights gained with the help of the fifth ray of Blue, as well as by the emotional control of the fourth ray of Blue. We need to be in charge of our emotions in order to dispassionately examine our faults. The fifth ray of Blue increases our sensitivity to them and, along with the fifth ray of Green, opens us to the God-power within us through the universal vibrant force entering our lives.

As we reach the awareness of these fifth rays, we learn that we can be reborn out of the conditioned, the unforgiven and the poor attitudes into the victory of the Christ love. With this rebirth comes the desire to forgive, to change old habit patterns and to strengthen positive attitudes, loosing from us the old garments that have bound us.

We begin to rely more heavily on the higher will, that will to do God's will. Evidence of spirituality is expressed in daily life — daily life becomes a spiritual exercise. Our dependence on the higher aspects of life brings its fruit of clear thinking and pure purpose as well as comprehension of dreams and visions. Growth has opened the door to the beginning of wisdom.

We are in no way through with the tests and struggles. That little ego still demands to be heard. It rides, it pushes, it wants more. But there rises in the soul-awareness the conscious need for victory over the little ego. With the appearance of the eighth ray of Blue, "divine force beautifies and modifies the tone of life, subduing the ego to some extent". The soul seeks greater development and the determination to follow the spiritual way increases. Help is ever at hand.

The search, the deep examination brings truth of ourselves and a realization of our growth. Thereby, with the help of the ninth ray of Blue, there is less confusion. We have at last come out of spiritual adolescence into adulthood. We are deeply appreciative of life and filled with the love of mankind. This love for mankind has finally overcome bigotry and the "don't confuse me with the facts, I've made up my mind" stubbornness of the heavier rays. The life is Christ-centered, full of compassionate understanding and love, not dependent on the outer because the inner life is so full.

Receptivity to this inner life is heightened, and awareness and conscious understanding expand to bring through the higher soul wisdom which has emerged to replace the old ego-centered concepts. Getting self out of the way brings a measure of spiritual balance, leaving more room for the inflow of God-power to aid in discernment and for increasing intuitive powers.

How does this affect our expression in life? Our capacity to love unconditionally deepens. Old patterns, old molds are broken and swept away. We have freed ourselves to walk the way of Love. Growth has matured, aided by the developing action of the eleventh ray of Yellow. We have learned to make the best of any circumstances and we are considerate and thoughtful of others' needs, a far cry from the self-centeredness of the second ray of Green.

The tenth ray of Red is the maturing and fulfilling of the eighth and ninth rays. We are at last ready to stand alone. We can lead or follow, go it alone or work with a group. It matters not. To serve is what is important. We are surer of ourselves and our relationship to life, this life and life eternal. We have gained strength, more than that shown in kindliness and self-sacrifice. From whence does this strength originate? All the ninth rays, and the eighth and tenth rays of Yellow are clues. We have both the warm receptive rays and the cooler rays of active strength that the ninth ray of Blue and the tenth ray of Green give. The potential power of the first ray of Red has become an actuality.

The growth that has matured and expresses as love tempered by spirit converts the nature to a totally spiritual expression towards our fellowman. Mother Teresa comes to mind, one unified with the Christ within. There is no need for approval from others for the power and support come from within, reflecting in the aura at-one-ment with Self and with God. The spiritual life is more fully lived each day. There is less of self, more dwelling on others' needs expressed through tenderness and concern for a brother.

This ray, the eleventh of Red, expresses the maturity of the eleventh ray of Yellow in all of life. It brings the development of humility. It contains self-effacement and forgetting of self. At-one-ment with God and illumination follow, though bits and flashes may already have been experienced. By mastering the little ego, the higher Self has recognized and merged with God's will. "Thy will be done, not mine." This at-one-ment lifts us out of the desire body into balance, serenity and power. With it comes a <u>conscious</u> realization of the oneness of the visible and invisible worlds and the realization of man as a spiritual being. This experience of fourth-dimensional consciousness occurs in many ways. The spiritual voice is stronger because we consult it more often. We enter within and receive the answer. We live in this Presence and find it blessing us wherever we are. We have a universal concept of life. We have tolerance and understanding. We look for and see the Christ in each one we meet, however briefly.

And what is yet to come? More growth. Greater refinement of the rays. A vision of Godhood. High resolve. Inward strength. And our auras gleam with the irridescence of all the beautiful color rays our Creator has provided, and our lives express this irridescence in service.

Chapter 4

PUTTING COLOR TO WORK

> The largest measure of benefit to every student who receives this training comes to him as a result of the personal effort he puts forth in the solution of his problems.
>
> Mary D. Weddell

The first time you are aware of color as an active energy you can use and relate to knowledge given in this book, you have begun to put color to work in your life. The first time you surround yourself with a specific color, you begin to put color into action. The first time you choose to wear a certain color to meet the need of the day, you have found another way of using and sharing color. When you mentally visualize a specific helpful color around another person, you are sending a color prayer. These first efforts can be the beginning of a wonderful adventure in living and in spiritual development.

Achieving greater awareness of the color surrounding you is an important step in applying color knowledge. Observe the colors in nature — the many colors in a sunrise or in a sunset, the soft to deep greens of shrubs and trees, the brilliant hues of flowers, the heart of a lily or a rose, the bright or muted colors of birds or animals. Observe soap bubbles as you wash dishes, the clothing people wear, their eyes and complexion. The Creator gave us beauty everywhere, an abundance of meaningful color.

A proven method of increasing conscious awareness of color is to take one color from this book and make it your own. You might, for example, concentrate on the color of Joy for a week, always associating the color with its meaning. Look for it in your home, your work environment and in magazine ads, stores, on television and in nature. Try wearing a touch of it. After becoming visually aware, notice how you feel when you see or wear your color. Take another color the following week. Awareness of feelings and thoughts concerning colors increases your sensitivity to them and will add to your spiritual development.

Much can be accomplished by using one color at a time. Later, however, you will be shown how to construct a complete color prayer plume.

One approach to choosing which colors to emphasize is to make a personal inventory by asking yourself such questions as: What are my strengths? What is my heart's desire? What are my personal, social, financial and spiritual goals? What steps am I taking toward them? Which Color ray qualities would help me to attain my desires and goals? Writing out your answers to your questions will help you to measure your progress.

A further step in acquiring awareness of and sensitiveness to color is the daily practice of meditation, for meditation aids in growth and self-development. Seeing color is often experienced in meditation and dreams. This is a realization of color action in the soul and, through the soul, to the aura which penetrates through and surrounds the physical life even as food digested in the stomach feeds man's whole being. Color prayer directed to the soul-center will be applied by it to the appropriate area. If you see color in your inner field of vision during meditation, mentally note it and later look up its meaning. As you persevere in this, you will connect with Universal Energy and receive answers to your needs.

The following brief notes will add to your general knowledge of color and guide you in beginning your exploration of how Color can benefit you.

Green gives energy, opens channels for growth, and is the ray of accumulation. Too much green without the balance of other colors will accent the ego. Use a rich, vibrant dark green as the base for color prayer plumes because it is energizing and is the tie-in between earth and heaven.

Blue contributes to an overall condition of calmness and serenity. Blue is soothing to the nerves and brings spiritual awareness. Its deeper hues will stimulate will power, self-control and right action. A cool color, it can chill or even depress if overused or not balanced with complementary rays.

Yellow is uplifting. It enlightens. It stimulates the intellect. Yellow helps to clear one's thoughts and to assimilate knowledge. Yellow is also health-giving. Yellow and orange foods are good to enliven the nerves. The sun's benefits are well-known.

Red helps to stimulate vitality and change. The magnetic current of Red is the basic Creative Life Force, vitally important to the aura of man. (Because red is a highly stimulating color red must not be used for any excitable condition nor for heart trouble nor high blood pressure.) All the Roses and Pink colors express different aspects of Love.

Purple soothes the mind. Purples in general bring a good balance to the life, a balance that comes from the depths and reaches the heights.

Light Gray is the color between colors of the aura.

Black, the absence of light, absorbs all colors.

White light is the presence of all colors. It is very strong. In Creative Color we use its components.

To summarize the general meanings and uses of color, one can say that the greens energize and stimulate growth, the blues contribute to an overall calmness and ego control, the yellows encourage enlightenment leading in time to illumination. The reds stimulate impetus to change, and the purples bring one spiritual balance, harmony and peace.

Because your thoughts, desires and feelings create the changing pattern of your everyday life, and these conditions reflect colors in the aura, well chosen colors can erase from the aura those qualities that are holding you back. It is the application of positive colors that cleanses and heals negative tendencies. An in-depth study of the psychological rays presented in this book can assist you in this process.

The balance of this chapter contains specific instructions on how to apply Color. By following these instructions you can integrate the knowledge you have gained, enhance the quality of your life and ensure progress in spiritual development.

USING THE INNER CHANNEL

The Inner Channel (Plate 1), is a safe, lighted pathway to spiritual development. It is, therefore, a good way to begin a meditation. You may have another method which works well for you. The terms "using" and "climbing" are interchangeable.

As explained in this volume, your own Inner Channel is a spiral of etheric substance centered within you at the solor plexus. Each color gives uplift and support to the spiral above it. Because each succeeding color is of a higher vibration than the one below it, you truly "climb" in consciousness while ascending the Channel. Each time you do so a little more color is added to your own etheric spiral, and you grow.

This is one way to use the Channel. Assume a comfortable meditative position. Take a few deep, easy breaths. Look at the Channel illustration. Then, beginning with the purple at the bottom, proceed upward, and audibly or silently name each color, its function and meaning as printed at the right of the colors. The words are:

I stand in the royal purple of Faith and mount to the gray lavender of the Holding Force of Patience, the pink lavender of Inspiration, the rose lavender of the Spiritual Voice and the blue orchid of Prophecy, over the yellow bridge of Enlightenment to the rose orchid of the Message Bearer, the red lilac of the Holding Force for the Band of Teachers, over the bridge of yellow Enlightenment to the glowing peach of Union of Mind and Spirit, the light blue orchid of Brotherhood, the blush orchid of Serenity, over the bridge of lightest green in Desirelessness to the rose bisque of Grace and the light blue lavender of Peace.

As you proceed, draw each color to the Inner Channel of your being. A focus of one or two seconds on each one, in turn, is sufficient. Keep relaxed during the process. You may prefer a short version of the words such as, "royal purple of Faith, gray lavender of the Holding Force of Patience," etc.

At the word "Peace", rest in the quietude of your lifted spirit in silent expectancy. This is a time of communion with the Infinite. Mary Weddell often reminded her students, "There is great value in the Silence".

If busy thoughts or pictures cross your mind, merely see them momentarily and let them go by. If you happen to see or sense colors while in the silence, jot down a brief notation, then attempt to duplicate them after your meditation is completed. More information on this follows in the article on Auric Viewing. In whatever way you imagine the Channel — as a ladder, a column of light, spiral stairway, etc. — absorbing the colors is what is important.

The length of time you stay in the silence will vary. At first one or two minutes may suffice. About fifteen minutes is usually the longest recommended time.

The faithful practice of the Channel, twice daily, is suggested for steady progress. A summary of the benefits that are possible through this practice is given in Chapter Two. The strength obtained through the use of the God-given Inner Channel helps to sustain your developing aura. The more you build these Channel colors and their qualities into your consciousness, the more you are able to sustain your growth.

Climbing the Inner Channel is also very effective in all types of meditations. For instance, if you have a question that needs an answer; or if you wish to meditate on a word such as "Love" or on a certain color; or if you have an urgent request, try presenting your need or word before entering the Channel. Release it when you reach the top. Then maintain the silence for a time, knowing with faith and gratitude that your answer or response is coming.

The answer may come in any one of many ways. You may open a book to just the right word. Answers may come in dreams or visions. In a telephone conversation you may hear yourself, or another, speak words of unexpected wisdom. An idea "out of the blue" may come while you are walking, or driving a car. You may experience a sudden tingling sensation together with "knowing" or "hearing" the needed information. While washing dishes you may find inspiration in the reflected color seen in soap bubbles. A paragraph in a newspaper or a line of dialogue in a television program may seem to have been inserted just for you. You may receive your answer immediately or days later. Gratitude for the answer stimulates growth in your soul.

Climbing the Inner Channel feeds the highest faculties of your inner being and increases your Christ Consciousness.

HOW TO EXPERIENCE AN AURIC VIEWING

An auric viewing is a meditation during which you ask for colors in your inner field of vision, expect to see or sense them in some way and record them on paper with pigment. Its purpose is twofold: (1) to develop spiritual insight for soul growth and (2) to develop a growing sensitivity in the higher senses, which are the spiritual counterparts of the five physical senses.

In the words of Miriam Willis, "An auric viewing will reveal you to yourself more and more clearly. The colors that you see are God's secrets revealed to you. They are filled with meaning. The form does not matter.

"Enter the silence with faith, desire, love, expectancy, and accept what the Spirit gives you. Also put down what you sense, if that happens. We can get vitality and power by the recognition of what we sense. If you 'feel pink' or 'purple' or whatever, put it down. It will act as a trigger, and you may then find that knowledge will follow. If you do not put it down you have blocked it.

"You may feel it is just imagination. It may be, but in putting it down you are clearing it so that the Spirit can come in. It will help you to grow in the spirit, and it is through knowledge of ourselves that we grow in compassion for others. We overcome criticism by knowing ourselves.

"We have in us 'the Christ within,' the divine spark. It is a potential. Through our meditations and seeking that spark has grown and we want it to grow even more. This growth is the union of the universal with the personal inner. Although this 'inner' is peculiarly our own, when we go within we obtain expansion and we obtain the universal.

"We must all function at the level of our development. Find your right place. Fulfill it and be ready for change because in this development you will find that the very chemistry of your body will change. This is very, very gradual. There are no cataclysmic shocks in our development. There are no psychic phenomena. We are not developing psychic power in the outside, emotional areas. Those are good when in their right place. This teaching is seeking to bring you beyond that into the Christ-power within. It is the spiritual path of Color, which is the very Inner Channel of your being. Whatever level you are, you will grow to a greater level if you will apply yourself. You have to do your own growing. You have to attain through your own experience."

Four Ways of Receiving Color

It has been found that placing a two-inch rectangle of forest green at the bottom of the page, followed by a narrow strip of sunlight yellow to bridge the color that follows, facilitates the auric viewing process. Refer to Diagram 2 (page 111) and see later portion of this chapter, titled "Entering the Silence and Recording the Colors".

People receive colors differently. Four ways of receiving color are described as follows:

DIAGRAM OF A COLOR PLUME*

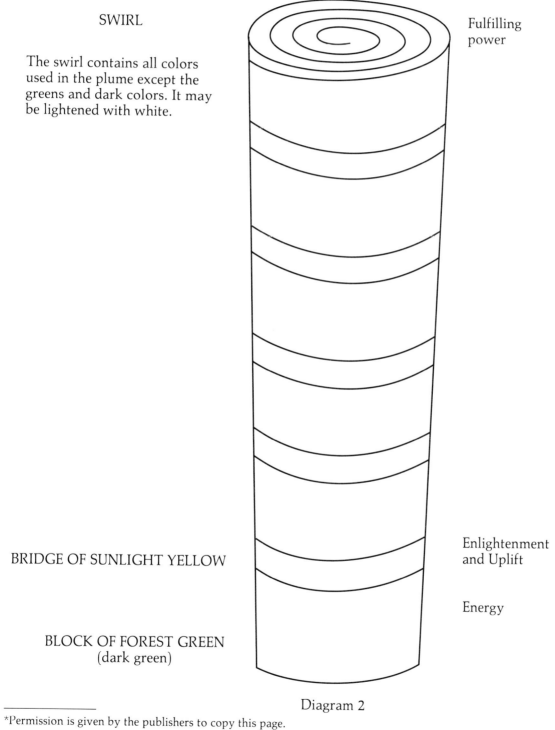

SWIRL

The swirl contains all colors used in the plume except the greens and dark colors. It may be lightened with white.

Fulfilling power

Enlightenment and Uplift

Energy

BRIDGE OF SUNLIGHT YELLOW

BLOCK OF FOREST GREEN
(dark green)

Diagram 2

*Permission is given by the publishers to copy this page.

<u>Tactile Method.</u> Rest in the quiet Peace at the top of the Channel, a symbol of man's reach to his Creator. Now let your hand feel for a crayon and place the color it is drawn to choose on the page above the bridging color of the sunlight yellow of Enlightenment. Now reach for another crayon. Place this color also on the page, above the first one made, as though you were building a column, block upon block, leaving a space between the colors for bridges to be added later. Trust this intuition and continue until you feel guided to stop.

Some people continue the tactile method for many months or longer, or come back to it from time to time as a preferred method because they find it a reliable way to circumvent a very active mental mind.

<u>Sensing Color.</u> Some people have an inward sensing of color. This, too, is a valid method. If you sense or "feel" a color, make a small notation of it. At the close of the silent time complete your paper as outlined in the tactile method description.

<u>Hearing a Color Direction.</u> Some hear, almost audibly, a color by name, number or meaning. This may occur rarely, regularly or combined with other methods. If you "hear" a color, make a notation and proceed as above described.

Do not be concerned if your active mind offers suggestions as well. Such a mind can usually be quieted if you gently but firmly tell it to be quiet for a time so that the higher mind can be heard.

<u>Seeing Color.</u> Some people see auric color, either with eyes closed or eyes open. Many see color almost immediately. It is very important, however, not to worry if you do not "see" at all. Through patience and persistence individual development will take place at the appropriate pace.

Several physically colorblind persons who have attended Color classes have been able to see auric color in their inner field of vision. They reported great satisfaction from the extra dimension of seeing that they experienced during the silence. They had trouble, however, in identifying crayons with their physical eyes, so used a tactile method, which worked well for them.

When one "sees," colors may appear singly or in a group, hold steady for a time or drift in and out of the inner field of vision. There are people who, in a state of elevated consciousness, see auric colors on the page, with eyes open. If you are one of these make an indication of the color and wait for the next. We can seldom duplicate with pigments the colors seen in light, but it is helpful to make the attempt.

Another way of seeing color is through concentrating on the color forest green. Make a block of dark forest green at least two inches square. Stare steadily at the green, taking in the color through your eyes. After a time you may begin to see colors shooting out from the green. These colors are being given to you. This method can be used to encourage "seeing".

Objects, people and forms in general, as well as abstract colors, may be seen during an auric viewing. Form is not relevant as far as auric viewing is concerned. Merely choose the dominant color or colors in each form, being sure to record both the dark and the beautiful colors. Accept what is given you and never strain. If you have a vision during meditation, record only the most outstanding colors. However, after your viewing is completed you would probably want to write about your vision and to draw some sort of representation of it. There may be an additional message in it for you.

Some people prefer to stay in the silence until they feel it is ended and then to record the colors in the order in which they remember them. Others make a scattered collection of colors during the silence, arranging them in sequence or other arrangement, completing the "blocks" after the silence.

Entering the Silence and Recording the Colors

During an auric viewing the physical body and the mental mind are quieted. People have used a variety of aids to raise their consciousness to a level receptive to color. Singing or playing recorded music has assisted many, and reading or listening to inspirational messages can be helpful. You may wish to record your own meditation tape.

In Creative Color Analysis the preferred method is to climb the Inner Channel immediately prior to proceeding with your own auric viewing.

Auric viewing colors are usually recorded in the form of a color plume, several of which are illustrated in this book. Please see the accompanying diagram also. It can be copied for your use. Color plumes are created from the bottom to the top and are begun with forest green. Green is a color of the magnetic field and forest green is the spiritual color nearest the earth in vibration. Through it you easily link your own vibration to the spiritual. The green gives you a necessary grounding and gives energy as well. Should your eyes tire, you can rest them by looking deeply into the dark green. Also, if you should happen to become distracted, looking into the green will help you to get back into focus.

A strip of sunlight yellow goes above the green to add enlightenment to its energy. These two colors open the soul to receive other colors. The yellow strip is called a "bridge". It is like a riser in a flight of stairs, or a half-tone in music. The bridge connects two colors of different rates of vibration so that they flow into each other more smoothly. You are now ready to record any colors received through any of the methods previously described. For your first auric viewings, if no other colors are given, you may use the yellow of enlightenment for all bridges. After a while you may feel guided to use additional colors.

The vertical column or plume arrangement of colors as described above is recommended because it facilitates the flow of spiritual power and increases the usefulness of the viewing. Other arrangements or methods which seem appropriate may be used instead. If you are using the vertical blocks, place a swirl at the top consisting of all colors seen except for the greens and dark colors. Blend the colors together with white. This aids in the absorption of the colors and their qualities. The swirl is the fulfilling power of the colors received.

Jotting down your feelings or impressions beside your colors, after you have placed them, can help you increase your awareness of your feelings and of your expression of them.

It is common for this whole meditative process to take less than twenty minutes, but follow your own inner direction. Guard against staying too long in meditation because it is important to keep in balance. Both the meditation and an expression of gratitude at the end, such as a simple "thank you" add power to the colors.

Interpreting and Using an Auric Viewing

After completing the auric viewing, a comparison between the colors seen and their meanings as represented in the Color Plates in this book will give insight into the experience. The colors given in an auric viewing reveal one's mental-emotional, physical and spiritual condition and may be given for one of several reasons:

1. To replenish or strengthen some quality which has become depleted, perhaps one you have recently overused.

2. To reveal or to help correct a problem, an undesirable condition or trait.

3. To reveal the possibility of a new spiritual quality, perhaps one you have deeply desired.

Every problem revealed is accompanied by a helpful color quality to assist in correcting or solving it. A color's personal meaning to you depends on its placement in relation to the other colors preceding and following it.

To receive the full benefit of the viewing be conscious of the reason for each color. Sometimes you will immediately know why a certain color was given. Also, if you ask yourself, "Why did I receive this color?" and wait a few seconds, often the answer will come. If it does not, you can study the book meaning of the color and search for a personal application therein. If you need still more enlightenment you can ask in meditation for further clarification.

Healing colors, faithfully applied, can help clear up situations, and they can help replace an unwanted trait with a desirable one. If you learn that a certain color is for replenishing, then you will want to "feed" yourself with that color at least twice a day for a week or longer. For example, if the color was the royal purple of Faith, you can imagine that color completely surrounding yourself like a soft cloud. You could look deeply into a color sample and draw it to yourself. "Breathing in" the color is another method of enhancing a quality. One person enjoys imagining a large, fully-lined cape of the desired color dramatically swung over the shoulders with a flourish. Another way is to affirm the presence of the color. For example, "I surround myself with the royal purple of Faith." There are, of course, many additional ways to use color beneficially.

Much good can come from meditating on one color a day from the auric viewing. If an indicated problem is health-related, you may want to take steps toward its healing or prevention.

Honesty with yourself in putting down colors, feelings and interpretations is a requisite for reliable results. One or two viewings a week with the accompanying study will bring progress. It is helpful to retain auric viewings, dated, in sequence, and to review them from time to time. It is revealing when reviewing to notice the changes in the colors as well as the repetitions.

As you become accustomed to and in tune with auric viewings you will often find a viewing to be a perfect color prayer for easing a situation which is causing you difficulty at that time. If you should find that your finished viewing has light colors at the bottom and heavier ones at the top, it may be that you saw the colors as they were reflected to you. Turn the paper upside down. If the sequence or reading feels more "right" to you, use the colors in that order. You may want to redo the viewing with the heavier colors at the bottom and the lighter at the top.

Additional suggestions to aid you in auric viewing include wearing beautiful, becoming colors and having beautiful articles nearby, such as a colored scarf, a vase of fresh flowers, or a fine painting. Let the God-center within be your guide.

HOW TO CONSTRUCT A COLOR PLUME

A color plume (color prayer or visual affirmation) is a sequence of color rays which flow harmoniously, as a full chord in music, from the lowest note to the highest. The purpose of a plume is to change a condition or to enhance a quality. Using the plume in Plate 6. To Reduce Tension, as an example, the following will illustrate one way to go about constructing a plume:

1. Begin at the bottom of the plume, as in all examples given, with a dark green. This color not only gives energy, it serves as the tie-in between earth and heaven. It enables you to use spiritual energy without depleting your physical energy.

    The strip or bridge of yellow above the green lifts you into the next higher vibration. It also enlightens, helping the mind to comprehend. This green and yellow are for the sender.

2. The first rectangle or block of color above the green and yellow is Consideration for Others, a soft blue lavender of medium intensity. Consideration for others helps lessen personal concerns and causes one to focus on the clearing of others' needs.

3. A bridge of Self Respect, a very pale pink-tinted orange, helps build respect for yourself and for others.

4. Next, the block of the royal purple of Faith gives spiritual energy to hold on to the respect and to know inwardly that the purpose of the plume, to reduce tension, can be met.

5. Above Faith is a bridge of rich gray lavender, the Holding Force of Patience. This helps you hold your faith firm and quiet.

6. You will thus be receptive to the blue lavender of Self-Revelation which can clarify the reasons for the tension. Something you can do to ease the situation can also be revealed, in a fresh perspective.

7. The bridge of Awareness, seafoam green, makes you aware of how to make use of the Self-Revelation to solve the problem. This may be at a subconscious level.

8. Because awareness can bring memories and excitement which arouse emotions, the next block, Power to Control Emotion, a soft grayed Wedgewood blue, is needed to control those emotions and thereby conserve the spiritual power you have been building.

9. Another bridge of Patience helps to centralize the emotions and maintain the control.

10. The deep rose to flesh color at the top of the plume can help you to overcome old habits, to activate and increase your capacity for loving and to develop respect for self and all men.

11. As you reach the top of the plume you mingle the <u>light</u> of your soul with the colors (all but the green at the base) by blending a delicate swirl of the plume's colors with white.

Each of the colors of this plume helps to eliminate the impediments to the free flow of creative energy and this helps to reduce stress and tension — the goal of the plume.

HOW TO USE A COLOR PRAYER OR VISUAL AFFIRMATION

Color is a healing agent which you can direct to a chosen purpose. Color is a non-invasive energy. When directed to another soul, the color is accepted only if that soul desires it. (If not accepted the color energy returns to the sender.) Early Color teachers taught their students to use color in specific ways, some of which are given in this book.

When you choose to send a color prayer, or use one for yourself, the following has proven effective:

1. Keep comfortably centered in and aligned with Universal Forces. You are sending color from your own soul center to that of another, or, if praying for yourself, infilling your own center.

2. Focusing on the dark green at the bottom of the plume, "breathe in" its vibrant energy, which is the energy tie from earth to heaven. Then "breathe in" the uplift of the yellow bridge. The green and yellow are for you.

3. Continuing to breathe in each color, mentally send this energy, color by color, from your soul center to the soul center of the recipient, or purpose for which you are praying. Naming each color's meaning as you send it adds to its effectiveness.

4. Send the color prayer, or visual affirmation, in complete faith and without strain.

5. Release your concern, knowing the energy is fulfilling its purpose. Then express gratitude in color or words to the Source of this catalytic healing energy.

6. Use a color prayer for about a minute at a time. Do this daily for a week or two and expect a change. Some conditions are alleviated more readily than others. You can safely repeat color prayers until the healing of the condition prayed for is accomplished.

If praying for a specific purpose, such as for world peace, just send the colors out from your soul center into the ethers.

QUICK COLOR REMEDIES FOR YOURSELF OR OTHERS

- For abdominal cramps — warm colors on the hands, place hands on abdomen

- To allow others their opinions — "clothe" yourself in old rose (12th of Red)

- For anger — blue green and lemon yellow

- For asthma — "clothe" the person in amber rose

- For backache — rose red to stimulate the circulation

- For balance — deep apricot

- For blood clot — old rose (and medical attention)

- For constipation — burnt orange, and hiss through the teeth as you draw the abdomen in and down

- For someone who habitually corrects another — rose orange with two stripes of turquoise blue placed diagonally within it

- For detachment in emotionally-charged situation — Wedgewood (cobalt) blue

- For difficult situation needing immediate action — salmon pink overlaid with burnt sienna (common sense) and/or rose red to coral pink (6th of Red)

- For emotional control — Wedgewood (cobalt) blue (4th of Blue)

- For energy when tired — look at the sky or think sky blue, or walk in or think of green grass or forest green, or think of rose red

- To calm excitement — gray and Wedgewood (cobalt) blue followed by burnt orange smoke, then lemon yellow to bring to reason

- To cool a fever — ice blue, alternate with dusty rose

- For forgiving self and others — deep rose (see 5th of Yellow)

- For frustration — moss green to gray blue to blue purple

- For color God bless you — see a waterfall's irridescent spray

- For headache — old rose to blue lavender, or seafoam green at back of the neck like a poultice, or ice blue on top of the head like an icebag

- For hemorrhoids — strong gray blue, follow with blue lavender, strong rose, then yellow

- To halt hysteria — deep gray blue with a rich red rose center

- For <u>indifference</u> — red rose and deep orange. Repeat. (Also see Psych. Green 1)

- For <u>indigestion</u> — Alternating deep green and rose stripes around affected part

- For <u>lassitude and weakness</u> — Creative life force (Psych. Red 6) to deep rose

- To stop someone <u>making fun of another</u> — red brown

- To quicken the <u>memory</u> for an exam — sun yellow around the head or rose gold and Wedgewood (cobalt) blue at solar plexus

- To stimulate the <u>memory</u> — a band of salmon pink about the head

- To <u>motivate</u> self or others — rosy copper (see Psych. Yellow 10)

- For <u>nausea, sick stomach</u> — Blue lavender to <u>ease and stop</u> vomiting OR rose orange to <u>induce</u> vomiting

- To lift above <u>pain</u> — ice blue, lavender and soft pink lavender

- For <u>patience</u> — dark gray lavender (darker than the Inner Channel patience)

- For <u>poisonous bite or snake bite</u> — silvery ice blue, blue lavender and get medical attention fast. Do not use green for it will increase the pain

- To stop <u>profanity or loud, noisy talk</u> — burnt orange smoke

- For <u>protection around your car</u> — Wedgewood (cobalt) blue with more gray in it, lined with rose

- For <u>scar tissue</u> — red with a shot of orange in it to rose orange. Alternate with blue rose lavender

- For a <u>sewing mistake</u> — lemon yellow

- To keep from <u>slipping</u> on ice, wet pavement or loose rug — burnt orange, orange and rose orange

- When giving a <u>talk</u> — stand in green energy

- For muddled <u>thinking</u> — Pick a color you like and spin in it for a while

- For positive <u>thinking</u> — bright blue (3rd of Blue)

- For sore <u>throat</u> — imagine an amber necklace, with emerald clasp at nape of neck

- For <u>tickle in the throat</u> — blue violet, follow with soft rose and blue violet

- To ease <u>whiplash</u> — smoky blue lavender for the nerves, then deep soft rose to stimulate the circulation

THE LORD'S PRAYER

Mary Weddell saw color on her hands as she played the piano. If she was singing, the colors varied with the words as well as with the harmonies of the music, so that each verse of a song had its own colors. "Every tone has its color, and every color has a tone," she taught. "Mary Weddell's Meditation On The Lord's Prayer" included here is her writing, wisdom from an illumined soul whose consciousness was vast. These lines proved to be her plan for living life.

The Lord's Prayer is so individual that each soul, each individual must interpret it for himself. There will be degrees of understanding of this prayer. Some will realize the universality of it. Others will apply it personally.

The colors in Plate Seven are those Mary saw on her hands when playing Malotte's "The Lord's Prayer" on the piano. They are appropriate for whichever translation of the prayer you use because the colors are a universal language. Mary's meditation helps to verbalize and define the height and depth of your own concept of a dedicated life. Each of you may find phrases therein which resonate to your inner being, and you may from time to time be inspired by them to envision new ideals and new life goals. Both the colors and Mary's meditation may assist you in recognizing and realizing ever deeper meanings in the prayer.

The colors and the meditation serve as two new approaches to increased understanding and appreciation of the Lord's Prayer. The color plate helps to develop intuition, the inner teacher. The meditation gives an exceptionally mature interpretation to ponder, and from which to make deductions regarding spiritual growth.

THE LORD'S PRAYER IN COLOR

Plate 7

Prayers in color are read from the lower edge up and from right to left. Combining the words with the color gives added meaning and power to the prayer. Singing the words produces even more power because music carries a still higher vibration. Begin at the lower edge of Plate 7 reading right to left, phrase by phrase:

<u>Our Father, which art in heaven, Hallowed by thy Name</u>. With these words you consciously open your soul to the sky blue of the Prayer Life Ray. Selfless prayers travel on this vibration.

<u>Thy kingdom come</u>. It takes faith to invite the coming of the kingdom, and the royal purple of Faith reinforces and magnifies the faith you are expressing.

<u>Thy will be done</u>. The color of Divine Imagination, rose purple, helps to open your consciousness to expanded vision. In an extended meaning one is asking that man may catch the vision of all the Good that the Universe has in store for mankind and the earth.

<u>On earth, As it is in heaven</u>. Azure blue is the color of fourth dimensional consciousness. It helps you to be conscious of the high vibrations of the invisible worlds and to bring down ideas and good from on high; those which Divine Imagination has envisioned and thus made man receptive to. If you prefer the "Heaven-within" concept, the color helps to bring spiritual ideals into earth living.

The yellow bridge of uplift gives added energy to the one saying or singing the Prayer.

<u>Give us this day our daily bread</u>. The chartreuse of Supply reminds you that "daily bread" means that which is necessary for your sustenance and needs at all levels. You acknowledge that this Supply is ever at hand, that God is the Source, that all is yours for the asking and that you need to ask in order to receive.

<u>And forgive us our debts, As we forgive our debtors</u>. For forgiveness of self and others the next row of colors begins with a color combining the gray lavender of Patience with the lavender of Self Revelation. Patience is needed in order for supply to materialize. It is needed to calm yourself so that with the color of Self Revelation you may see clearly your faults. Then ask for an infilling of God's great Love, rose, to cleanse faults from your soul and aura. So long as one harbors ill will against another, in any form, the aura will not be clear, nor can one do one's best work for the Kingdom. Therefore, the phrase regarding forgiving others is extremely meaningful. The rose also carries the meaning of asking forgiveness. The yellow following the rose strengthens your endeavor to keep integrated by living according to spiritual principles. After a cleansing it is important to infill with good. The yellow infills.

<u>And lead us not into temptation</u>, Temptation is the color at the right side of the next row above. It is similar in color and meaning to Envy and Discontent.

<u>But deliver us from evil</u>. The clean, clear emerald green follows immediately after Temptation. This green carries the meaning of and energy for spiritual life present in the physical. You have previously, in this prayer, called on Higher Sources for ideas and asked that they be brought into earth manifestation. You have been assured of a goodly supply for all your needs, been cleared anew, through God's Love, of all evil thoughts toward yourself or others and received spiritual help to feel encouraged to persevere. The emerald green helps you to make use of all this good in daily living.

Known difficulties, however, may still be in the way so protection is needed. All of the spiritual good previously invoked is called on to help. The steel gray following the green is a protection from any harm you might encounter. When used as a shield it effectively protects you from any unwanted vibrations from outside yourself. This is sometimes referred to as "putting on the armor of God".

<u>For thine is the kingdom, and the power, and the glory, forever</u>. The three lavender colors in the next line above include the meanings of Power, Harmony, Peace, and something similar to Self Revelation and Loving Compassion-with-Patience. They are untranslatable as individual colors.

<u>Amen</u>. The top part is the "Amen" or "So be it". It contains a great uplift. You are free to make this Amen as glorious, as uplifting, as colorful as you feel.

MARY WEDDELL'S MEDITATION ON THE LORD'S PRAYER

OUR FATHER

Thou, Who art the IMAGE OF PERFECTION in me and in all things.

In Heaven

Who, through the LAW OF BALANCE, creates a harmonious vibration in my mental body which gives me strength, through the knowledge and power of THY WILL, to keep all confusion or weak, negative thoughts out, so that the LIGHT OF THE ARISEN CHRIST may shine through the physical body, removing all obstructions — those of fear, doubt, lack, or limitation.

Hallowed be Thy Name

I shall forever be conscious that I am ONE WITH THEE. In all things that I undertake to do, I shall, by THY POWER and through THY WILL, KNOW that it is the Father within who doeth all things, consecrating myself as a HOLY CHANNEL for you, GOD, to pour out YOUR blessings to all humanity.

Thy Kingdom Come

Through my BELIEF IN THEE, of whom I am now FULLY CONSCIOUS THAT I AM A PART, my thoughts are forever with the ONE THINKER, the ONE CREATOR, and I know only that state of happiness which is to be found in THE FINISHED KINGDOM. YOU through the LIGHT AND ILLUMINATION OF THE SPIRIT WITHIN, have opened the DOOR to the KINGDOM OF IMPERSONAL LOVE, and through this knowledge, have taken down the barriers of human limitation, and made it possible for all to enter.

Let Thy Will Be Done

As I take a stand for Truth, and as the vision broadens my understanding, I lose sight of the personal self, knowing now, that IF I want to create only good in my life, I must always be ONE WITH THE CREATOR.

I fully realize that no task is too small or too great for me, thy child, to accomplish, so long as I keep this state of consciousness, knowing that it is not I, but YOU, through your DYNAMIC POWER, who can lead me into the HIGHEST GOOD. Whatever I ask in THY NAME, so is it already granted.

As in Heaven, so on Earth

In reaching for the HIGH VISION, I fully realize that whatever is given to me from "THE SECRET PLACE OF THE MOST HIGH" can be brought back to my physical consciousness, and as it is the desire of the Heavenly Father to give His child the best in life when that child is ready to receive it, and enjoy all things to the highest good while on the physical plane, therefore, as I keep my balance, I can, through HIS WILL, as I see and hear the MASTER'S talk, release myself from the shackles of human bondage, and while IN EARTH, have the same privileges as those IN HEAVEN.

<u>Give us Bread for our Needs Today</u>

Every day I MUST ENTER MY CLOSET AND SHUT THE DOOR. I must realize there is no past, and there is no future — there is ONLY NOW. As I live, moment by moment, I KNOW THAT GOD IS IN HIS HIGHEST HEAVEN, and ALL IS WELL. I am now receiving "MANNA FROM HEAVEN", and my every want is taken care of.

I have lost sight completely of the selfish self. I KNOW THAT GOD IS GOOD. I AM His expression of good and must live up to the highest ideals of that DIVINE PRINCIPLE WITHIN ME, AND I WILL.

<u>And Forgive us our Offenses</u>

<u>as we</u>

<u>have Forgiven our Offenders</u>

As I realize more and more the Power that you, GOD, have placed in this fleshly body, my plan of life will be "ALWAYS TO HELP, NEVER TO HINDER".

I will be patient, kind, loving and tolerant to all who have not found the illumined "ONE" within. I know that the physical part of me is not insensible to the sorrows and heartaches around me, with the physical eyes we do behold the "INTOLERANCE" in the world today. BUT, knowing now that "I AM" a part of "THEE" I shall never be a part of anything only that which is a "PART OF THEE". Therefore, I can freely forgive and forget anything that is said and done in an unkind and thoughtless manner.

I shall never forget that JESUS was the Conqueror of a "PSYCHIC" force that is destroying the world today. As He became "MASTER" of all things, so shall "I".

<u>And do not let us Enter into Temptation</u>

<u>but</u>

<u>deliver us from Error</u>

With this knowledge, and by THY WILL, nothing that is not God-like can tempt me "off the mountain top".

High thought, through the strength of THY WILL, as I am forever conscious of it, will never let me bow down to any will other than THINE. I AM ONE WITH THEE. Therefore, I need fear no thing. I am captain of my soul. YOU, GOD, are my port of safety. My course is clear, I see with the EYE OF SPIRIT, and no confusion can ever enter my life.

<u>Because Thine is the Kingdom</u>

I now realize that ALL GOOD is from THEE. I am but a Channel through which YOU work.

Each moment you are inviting me, your child, into the LIGHT, to come into a CONSCIOUS KNOWING that, as I control every rebellious instinct, impulse, and emotion, I live now in the KINGDOM OF GOOD.

<u>And the Power and the Glory</u>
> <u>for Ever</u>
>
> <u>and Ever</u>

I shall, from this moment on, seek glory, to glorify THEE, as I use YOUR POWER from the Infinite Storehouse of Supply. Everything I undertake to do will never be too small or too great, KNOWING THAT THOU ART WITH ME. I AM LIFE IMMORTAL.

Mary E. Weddell.

DR. GEORGE WEDDELL ON PRAYER

The natural cry of the inherent soul for expression and relief, in the multitudinous diversity, the endless obstacles and infinite craving for Light, is the true prayer of the traveler on the path.

He struggles and strains against the never-ending handicaps that are thrust in his way and when the weary soul needs comfort and encouragement it cries in prayer to the unknown but perceived cosmic consciousness for just a little help. Somehow and someway the clouds are lifted and the wings of faith and hope carry the votary onward and upward toward the eternal shore of light.

The pressing need of life is this attitude that recognizes a Cosmic Creator and a faith that He can be contacted by a humble spirit and proper perspective.

Prayer lifts the soul above the sordid and material and allows the spirit to travel in the ancient realms where it had its original source. The entanglements of matter are so tenacious in their hold upon our consciousness that it takes very often a grim determination to halt the senses and cast the eyes to the stars where hope lies.

Life moving through a dense vibration can only contact the Infinite by shutting from sight the evidence of the senses, hence, the attitude usually assumed by one in prayer. The natural inhibition of matter in its lower vibration almost stifles the aspirant and so inhibits that it often requires time to get in the proper mental and spiritual atmosphere.

But the spirit must reach out to its source and in this period of contemplation true prayer is accomplished. To repeat certain words without any emotion from them is worthless, as the effect of a prayer is directly dependent upon the amount of true devotion and aspiration that is in the soul at the time of the prayer. When the Great Master said "their prayers were as a sounding brass and tinkling cymbal" he referred to this great occult truth.

Prayer opens up a channel of force that flows straight from the throne of God, and the amount of help and strength we receive depends upon whether we are asking for Soul Development or not — this is dependent entirely upon the amount of self that permeates our petition.

When the soul transcends the boundaries of sense and passes to the realm of spirit, then one realizes that our sojourn here is truly only one transient in the extreme, and the true home is in that land of effulgent light where each radiates his own glory as a reflection of that grandeur of the Heavenly Father.

Prayer also recognizes our proper relation to the Creator and gives us pause that our vanities shall not obscure totally our vision and forever hold us from that radiant source of light and truth.

So let prayer be our buckler and shield that will anchor us to our Heavenly Father and pilot us safely through the maze of materiality and eventually land us in that home of radiant beauty and light.

Lift our hearts in prayer so that the scroll of the Heavens will be unrolled to you and the unknown will become known, the hidden will be revealed, and the ineffable sweetness of the songs of the spheres will break upon the soul consciousness, and the Heavenly echoes will transport us to a land of peace, free from all strivings where only abundant joy will be our bed of happiness and we will perceive the ultimate in God and His Universe.

May 25th, 1928

Chapter 5

MARY'S INSIGHTS ON COLOR

>Spirituality is not a luxury or a decorative appendage to be occasionally displayed. It is daily living in God's world of color in radiant faith . . . Every individual is a chemist engaged in working for perfection in the laboratory which is his own body.
>
>>Mary D. Weddell

Through the years Mary Weddell wrote comments on her students' auric viewing papers as she interpreted the colors. These insights express great wisdom. Her comments, unedited except for distinctly personal guidance, comprise this chapter.

* * *

Just as around our bodies there is a physical world from which we draw our physical strength, so around the auric channel is a spiritual environment in which we can live in <u>vital contact</u> and from which we can draw replenishment of power. Try testing this factually. Prove that your body can be relaxed at once no matter where you are or what you are doing. Prove that by relaxing your mind you can create a greater activity in the functioning of mind and body. This is well worth trying to accomplish by using the creative colors you are now aware of. You will find your balance and poise much stronger.

* * *

Faith finds God and enables the spirit to rest in Him, even while the mind keeps working in both doubt and fear of not truly seeing this mystery and the meaning of the auric channel. But faith in its innermost reality is not intellectual nor is it an activity. Faith is a state of spirit, a relationship to the spiritual world.

* * *

Faith, vision and sweetness of spirit are the creative forces that transform one set of conditions into color creating balanced power.

Color can and will develop intuition. Listen for the still, small voice, that which conveys the undeniable <u>conviction of truth</u> that neither reason nor persuasion can set aside. The intuition is a source of unlearned knowledge, a source of creative inspiration, a fountainhead of energy. It is God's creative and redeeming love ready to be poured upon every needy soul for healing. For perfect usage of color healing each soul must be empty of self and thirsty for this divine gift.

* * *

Test your growth in creative energy. Prove that your body can be relaxed no matter where you are and at the command of your will. First relax your mind. By so doing you release creative energy to be used in making contact with the higher mind. Eventually you find your mind functioning in the fourth dimensional plane. It keeps you in balance. This is well worth developing. Use color of release green for energy for practicing this.

* * *

The ultimate purpose in use of color is that through the channel we develop sight and hearing. This is the creative life lived in freedom.

* * *

When you correct your own color picture, try to think away from yourself, a mental exercise given to train teachers to think away from their opinion into the auric pattern of their students. To do this you must remember your way through controlled thinking. This is an act of <u>faith</u> in color. Come where the Eternal Spirit, Love itself, untangles, loosens and pulls away from you all that binds; walk as you would in a garden of roses, hear the fountains of goodness and the birds of joy singing. Use color in all ways possible.

* * *

We all have levels of color thinking according to the development or spiritual unfoldment. These differences in color symbolism arise from some kind of interiorness — the recognition of values — conscious, subconscious or unconscious.

* * *

Peace, patience, placidity, serenity, confidence, compassion are all handmaidens of <u>faith</u>, gained only through the periods of silence when one dwells in spiritual ecstasy while in communion with the Divine Spirit. Through the source of this mystic rhapsody we find the mystery of life. Sight and hearing are the result. Knowledge of the spiritual world is given in visions of color and the creative flow of energy an invisible pure force. And what is this creative power? It is the radiation of God's Love. Color is the symbol by which we become aware of development. This is to realize the color path in our daily life, the path Christ trod. We are then polarized with heavenly magnetism.

* * *

It takes time for the auric channel to be used. Chemical changes take place as our faith increases. The truly developed student learns to discriminate between the intuitive spiritual message that follows the creative power of the auric channel, and the mental message that can be given as a prophecy through clairvoyance. How then shall we live? By consciousness and with joy. Alertness is our watchword. Soon one can raise his vibrations to such a pitch that they increase beyond the ordinary thinking level and go seeing into the auric channel and come back enlightened.

* * *

Come alive with creative energy building up vibrations of health and happiness. As we center our thinking on still and quiet waters, we touch upon a vibration of peace fluidic and find we are flowing with the power. Thus we see the auric development supplying our needs. Rest then in Divine Suspension; bring the invisible into the visible. One is actually being in space by pure healing thought; release yourself from the sense of time and space. This, my dear, is worship without fear.

* * *

Development comes as a great cleansing wave. As it leaves the shore it leaves behind that which cannot be used. So, in your life you can discover for yourself your growth and that which you no longer need to support your desires. They become less as we develop the auric channel. Our responses are more spiritual and the consciousness of reality dwells with us. For effective prayer, faith is necessary. Visualize your heart's desire and place colors in operation. Make yourself one with Christ. You have looked into reality. Your staff is your faith. Your heart must be filled with love when you enter the crossroads of life and live in the fluidic powers of color.

* * *

Intuition as we see it, by its divination, is simply insight. A process as direct and swift as bodily vision. It is the exercise of the eyes of the intelligence, the unerring recognition of a truth presented on the mental plane.

It is with certainty its vision is unclouded, its report unfaltering. No proof can be given to these visions for proof is above reason. We have proven that by the use of the <u>Color Channel</u>. The illuminating pathway is shown through visions. The mind creates its own heaven. Color is proof to one who sees it. As with a flame we may light a wick and the color of the flame will depend on the nature of the wick and of the liquid in which it is soaked. So it is with the human aura and the depth of the illumination tells the reader of auras the nature and habits of the human being. If we read the aura of a person who is in a state of "civil war" within himself, a vortex of passion without self training, we see no evidence of the higher ego. The auric colors are strong and deep. If one becomes aware of emotions and finds true balance, the aura around him changes and the balance is reflected in the aura.

* * *

I feel lives can be enlarged in many ways if the person can become aware of the "Christ-life." To live the life of the spirit in the midst of the world's stress and strain is the hardest test. If one's life can radiate joy and let the basis of the reality be glorified by sympathetic understanding of mankind's needs, I believe that is the proof of our night work and our development.

* * *

The waters of life are yours for the asking. Are you using your supply daily as it is given you? <u>Be</u> a reflection at all times of the beautiful reality which is your night life. Worry leads also to that dreadful thing — petulance. Out of petulance grows stubbornness. Love enough that nothing will affright you for the basis of all <u>anger</u> is <u>fear</u>.

* * *

Find yourself a comfortable chair in a quiet room knowing the need to meet there. See him or her in every color of blue for a week and explain the meaning of the different shades of blue. Surrender to thy Divine Guidance. Bathe the person in the auric colors, relax and know these experiences can bring you illumination. And help you both to grow. This higher self lives not in the earthly but in the heavenly world.

* * *

To apply the practice of color, whether prayer or treatment, we must basically work out on a positive color. To apply this idea on ourselves is not an easy one. But if one can apply the color in teaching, holding the color as an expression of the universal mind, we gradually become aware of our spiritual directions; the spiritual nature operating within the creative center of our lives, we automatically resist and realize when things are not for us. The human judgment becomes a part of the divine reservoir of supply. What you are seeking will be yours. Thank you and may you experience this that is in store for you.

* * *

What do you want most? Have you thought on this fact? True loveliness in personality is the outward expression of the auric channel, the genuine beauty of God. Growth in auric viewing creates a stimulating ray that those who come into your presence will be stirred with a desire to become more spiritual. Being as you are, parts of spiritual essence and also of flesh, you are at this stage of your development tremendously influenced by what we call evidence of the senses. We express it thus: I see, I feel. I sense fourth dimensionally.

All that is asked is an awareness of God's awareness of you, His child, for once this knowledge becomes a part of you, your development is assured.

* * *

Use your imagination to realize that hidden strengths within you are awakened sometimes through great experiences or shocks, through losses or ill health, and with the courage that God gives we grow in faith. You have had instructions as to the opening of your auric eyes. And with the sustaining power of the Channel, you are now able to picture the lighted passage and its radiant colors; you have the chart; your course is laid. Turn into the eternal silence where love alone can open the flood gates of living waters. Hold yourself in a listening attitude and be an artist in Christ, letting color flood your path.

The first progress in Auric Viewing is prayer. Another requisite for progress is humility. Be aware of your creatic power and climb to higher ground each day. By listening, you will not make mistakes in your work. Your knowledge is great; you are expected to give it to another. Just step into the higher consciousness by the means that is easiest for you. Never strain. Let your mind think for a moment, then enter a sunrise and walk in auric power. See anything God has created and know it is good.

* * *

The auric life you reveal to me stands for many things attained through constructive thinking and like action. To me, gaining spiritual understanding is the challenge of our time. We do realize the deeper we sink our roots in faith the greater our knowledge of life becomes. We must learn to be listeners and as we listen to the story of a frustrated life we can flood that person with colors and something higher and greater than ourselves goes with that person. We can change lives through our creative knowledge of the auric channel and the guidance of Christ's life.

* * *

The color course brings us the knowledge of ourselves which often heretofore has been hidden and shows us how necessary it is to carry our share of a brother's load. Color also can help us to know when to hand back the load to another for fear that he may grow to expect help that the future cannot supply. Thinking becomes a burden. Your capacity for helping in time of need has given you development and we hope color comes to mean as much to you as it does to us.

* * *

Within the heart and the knowledge of right decisions, ease of mind becomes greater. Growth, love, wisdom and power are given to use as a symbol of devotion to Christ and His infinite Love. Always the power of imagination helps us to enter the field of prayer and from there into the auric channel. There, every color is ours for the asking. Color is healing and peace comes.

Color is an accomplishment with a permanent ray built into your Auric Channel.

* * *

Faith finds God and enables the spirit to rest in Him even while the mind keeps working in doubt and seeing in both mystery and meaning. Faith in its inmost reality is not intellectual nor is it an activity. Faith is a state of the spirit, a relationship to the spiritual world.

* * *

For good results in color healing, each soul must be emptied of self and thirsty for the Divine gift of creative power. The supply comes through the auric channel. The auric colors can develop intuition which conveys that undeniable conviction of truth that neither reason nor persuasion can set aside. Intuition is the fountainhead of creative ability. The auric channel is your power line from God.

Use a robe of lavender for tranquility of spirit and to relax mental strain.

Pink rose and blue are twin rays of harmony.

* * *

The flowing out of God's color demands the flowing back. Harmonics in color intensify the power of creative force, thereby holding healing power longer for benefits to the one in mind. As one can be drawn by music, so can one be drawn by color. Ego cleansing by knowledge is to your advantage. If your mind becomes troubled it is not your mind, it is your desire body. You can very wisely change by an energized auric plume of humility and peace.

* * *

Apply all color treatment in faith and think it will be healing and peace-giving to those in need. Realization of this truth will bring greater power to you.

* * *

A promise of the communion or "Cup of Christ" identifies you with your longing to know peace.

A soul can be very satisfied if fed by harmonious surroundings. Self pity has been used as a crutch; this is really lack of respect for self, often a fear unanalyzed. With knowledge of color applied this can be overcome and self-control assured and a quality of peace gained beyond that which has yet been experienced.

* * *

Your house is now dedicated. It is a shrine, as it were, where events of the higher place will come to pass. Your order is good, your house is ready as a setting for the enticement of souls. Your house is a way station for all sorts of travelers who will sense in you the peace and creative power that is indwelling there. You are a personal representative of "Christ's teachings," and must do the tasks His will sets for you. To do this is a very meager explanation of a rich tapestry of what the spiritual color course has done for you and what living the color life will continue to do for you.

* * *

To him who lives in Spirit all resources are his and life is a trust. It is the most priceless, the most infinitely valuable possession — a gift of rare power and unlimited resources, this gift we are given by becoming possessed by color, applying the Creative power of the Channel to our everyday living. This has been given you for a time of reflecting and rebuilding. You have received into your life through Color the Creative power of recharging, and making more perfect your household affairs. We ask you not to return to old forms of thinking. Do not panic but slowly accomplish — your house and clothing will take on a new radiance and you can be directly responsible for better health for yourself and family.

Three great tools to work with in color are Love, prayer and joy. Joy is a companion we so often lack. Joy is the first law of life. We must learn this law. Joy is fundamental praise of God. It is a way, a road, a lane or an avenue. Travel its length and breadth. It is never too late to learn to use it. Eat joy as nourishment. Live it in color. It will multiply as doth the mustard seed and bloom sweeter than the rose.

* * *

Progress on earth is from almost unconsciousness in infancy to wisdom in ideal maturity. Progress on the Spiritual Planes is no different. You are already in the upper oval of earth wisdom as you are using color, going in and out of the Channel. The real significance is your willingness to use color to help others. The first requisites of color attainment are humility and prayer.

* * *

Be a little more self-indulgent. Dress your body with colors that will improve your health. Do not go too far in self-denial. We ask this that you may more easily work in color. Happy is the one who has attained the knowledge that the body is the spirit's shadow on the green earth, and that the form of this shadow reflects the sun of life. The psychic senses through color are developing by the realization of universal consciousness. It can become a conscious development through the Channel.

I feel the absence of criticism means the presence of love. And love is the fulfilling of a natural law. If we truly revere that which is above and beyond us, we are living within the law of mystical surrender. Our life is created by our thinking if it goes off its course. Thought is vibration that etches a picture upon the sensitive plates of the brain.

* * *

This channel by which you are judged is developed by auric viewing. As we go further we realize it is a power of creative energy on the fluidic force of God's love, helping us to know Him.

The creative power has a will of its own and free will was given to mankind to be able to use this divine force. As pupils of color we become intimate with the reason for our lives and conscious of the purpose of this gift of living in a mightier realm of understanding. As the chemistry of our bodies and the Channel changes we become aware that our own little selfish desires have taken wings. Then religion is always mystical. As we develop the divine force love answers all.

* * *

Be alerted to the strength you have offered to you. When your mind ceases to race and has this vital energy shown you and all thought is erased for a moment in that stillness, then you revert to the basic being "God" created in His image. He answers prayer and solves your life's problems, and each energized form of "greens" in this picture reminds you of what you have overcome by entering His Kingdom. Forget all those errors committed against you by others who lacked understanding. Give thanks!

Balance is the vibrant note in the theme of your development. According to my judgment, in your case the three bodies of desire must become as a sleeve within a sleeve and as you continually operate in this harmonic vibration, you would realize the chemistry of your body was changing thereby balancing the glands of your body and opening a new area of consciousness. You are accomplishing this delicate balance.

* * *

Our bodies are servants of our minds. Some of us are slave drivers, our concept being we can always rest and rebuild, this many times is sadly in need of some outside support. I know a doctor has more knowledge than I could possibly have, that is a source of supply. I know prayer is Creative and healing power. I add colors and have stepped up creative power. I believe the Lord's Prayer is no mysterious incantation; it is the exercise of the divine activity of mind in the correction of human ills. A color prayer brings us into direct action of God's world of Divinity. To successfully see spiritually we must shut out the physical world. The Channel is the pathway to the kingdom within. God bless you. We all love you. Mary

* * *

It is on the wings of aspiration for perfection that the student soars into the Channel vibrations, attains union with the Higher Self and by virtue of the colors he expressed we know the chemistry of his body is changed. He then can know reality.

* * *

As a result of your night work your visions will give you a working power, and we suddenly realize we are making a conscious transition from our material mask into a spiritual stronghold. You make this transition. No one can make it for you. Have you thought of human life being very like the echo of our beloved childhood? We have spoken mockingly, angrily, joyfully and lovingly and back upon us have echoed the reverberations exactly as we sent them out. We live in a world peopled by our own thought images — not a joy we can trace back to the faith and aspiration which we long have cherished. Emerson said, "My dear children of life's highway, you will meet nothing you were not meant to overcome. Vision is perception; understanding and demonstration must follow before it becomes an established state of consciousness."

* * *

Scientists claim in the study of vibrations worlds within worlds within worlds are disclosed. The scale runs from dense low vibrations of seemingly solid material through finer and finer worlds. As innumerable voices fill a room at the same time, each voice however maintaining its distinct individuality, so with sense eyes we think we see ourselves following a course in life where man can impose his seeing and eventually knows reality, or Infinite Mind. In our Channel, auric messages have caused many a life to change and some who have received Cosmic Consciousness have found life's fulfillment. There is immense spiritual value and discipline in viewing the Auric Channel with a class. You are one in mind and the power is given all in right relationships, as in an intimate prayer group. The insight into reality or truth takes away nervous tension.

* * *

The radical change which occurs when we are born into the Heaven life; the searching analysis to which we are subjected; the desire of things earthly all have to become submerged into a true desire for spiritual adjustment. This is not a passing thing but a complex host of physical desires.

* * *

Renunciation is a great need in preparing to live in God's reality. A gate leads out of the Lighted Passage through an open door into the Auric Channel. This door is visible in auric viewing only to those who pass through the gate. This gate is self-renunciation. After working in this color course everything cries out in us, "We must renounce." When we have acquired the idea of the truths given us in these viewings, and put our lives in order, we soon know by the singing sweetness within, "Of myself I am nothing." It is the God within, this Faith manifested in Grace.

* * *

Healing is obtaining the single eye which makes the body full of light and our affairs transparent and beautiful. Healing is the revealing of the perfect body through the revelation of the path of Color. The Kingdom within. Healing is the discovery of our original selves, through the disclosure that is given us in Color Viewing.

* * *

We find after our study of the Auric Channel the order of our lives is in the expression of the ideal given us through the Infinite, when we entered this earth life. The moment the disclosure of this ideal is restored we find a Cosmic experience attuned to our night work and that work sustained by the neophyte during his day. The desire for things is submerged in the desire to serve in God's world where man must find the answers.

* * *

Transcribed from the Sanskrit: "Four men stood before God at the end of the seventh day. The first man said, 'What is it for?' The philosopher he. The second man said, 'Why did you do it?' The scientist. The third man said, 'Let me have it.' The barterer. The fourth man said nothing, but fell down and adored and when he arose he made one like it . . . The artist. Open my eyes that I may see."

* * *

In the secret chamber of each soul is hidden an intense desire for beauty which is the perfection of the spiritual world. The ability to produce our own visions into tangible results is the power of faith. Faith steps out into unseeming void and finds solid rock. Faith is an insight into the Mind of the Creator. A real experience is one in which we are conscious of God's love and power. Spiritual experience is the recompense which is never lacking if we keep the sustained contact with the invisible helpers knowing we in turn can through prayer and meditation send forth Creative power from the Auric Channel. Love guides us through the darkest night and causes us to see God in every man.

I see you have been given the light of understanding. That should be a vital promise for healing. If you have received this light your intuition will be an asset in helping people. New wisdom will make your mind come alive with the beauty of creation, for color is the reflection of the revelation of God in you. The nearest way to describe the Auric Channel is as a refined essence of Spirit. If you could distill thought you would get near this refinement. So human thought cannot find words to express the silence that presses through the lighted path, the stillness of a sunset seen from a great height, a silence that one is held in, and he knows for sure the inspiration of the "Presence." That, my dear, is the "height of understanding" and Christ said, "What I tell you in the darkness, that speak ye in light."

* * *

I see you have on your paper aspiration, following you have the urn of life, with the holding force of the fourth ray of blue; a very true example of growth . . . Color cannot give its power if the channel is not developed.

When you are accustomed to going in and out of the Auric Channel you will find viewing has a vitalizing effect on your body. These treatments in color will contribute to an overall condition of calmness, of conscious awareness of your needs.

For refinement of spirit and desire to please, use green.

* * *

Established character is the capacity to receive and the ability to obey. Those who have natural discretion of character must guard against being too positive in their opinions, for spiritual man is not aggressive. He who has had spiritual revelation does not need to fight. He knows with certainty and he can well bide his time, until revelation comes to others. As those who have crossed a stream we must patiently wait for others to do the same, with confidence in their ability because of their heritage. All growth is dependent on stimuli. We are using color as our stimuli. The Lighted Passage follows the "Eight-fold Path" of the seeker. The vision may come to anyone, but it abides only with him who can recognize its revelation. By our faith in the Auric Channel and our proof through Viewing we solve our problems and find peace and happiness.

* * *

If we can become centered in God or the creative life, we naturally become aware of the opening of the secret desire chamber that is hidden in each soul, a desire for knowledge. Eventually we know our intense desire for beauty is a reflection of the spiritual world. We feel ourselves invested with a divine mission and with spiritual insight through the Channel.

* * *

Personal response to color causes one to become aware of all creation in color. If you are of a color meditative nature you will stay to some of the softer blues. You usually choose the colors that harmonize with you. Some colors excite a person, others have the power to soothe. Unhappy experiences may cause one to withdraw from some color that would be healing to another. As you go forth into the Auric Channel your experience in Auric Viewing may be equal to a sunset that will mean only the awakening of clearer vision.

For rising joy use the oranges. You cannot find a spot in God's world that doesn't express color. Your color is an expression of you and your inner life.

* * *

Cosmic glimpses are borne in upon us in moments of quiet relaxation. Transformation through growth in the auric teaching gives us knowledge of chemical transmutation. As the yeast changes the composition of meal so that it is another composition from that which it was before. And to be aware of these changes take away limitations and we are living in Creative color with universal vision. Working in the Light of vision we find a comradeship of true friends and helpers, those who stimulate and inspire us to the outreach of our creative minds. Color is what we have engraved upon our consciousness through seeing the invisible which becomes invisibly visible, as we become more faithful in keeping our tryst with the lighted Channel.

* * *

Love is revelation. Have you thought of this? Even the simplest life has many departments. In the light of love we take an inventory of these and build into each our ideal of what it should be. This can be done with a perfect expression if we permit truth to interblend and so color our thinking.

Love is the infallible weaver of destiny. To know truth is to live in the Creative power of God's love.

* * *

Faith uncovers the real self and we stand revealed to ourselves and to our fellow beings. God has always known the possibilities of each for we are His own. But faith enables us to know through the Channel that we can develop and express the innate gift with which we are endowed. The vision of faith is shown in your work. Former beliefs and limitations are passing away as color and creative life renew you. For demonstrations of colors in viewing the Channel would ensure you of a happier life.

* * *

Ignorance is a vacuum to be filled with knowledge. The body of man is the outcome of his consciousness. Legs and arms are his registered beliefs in his power of motion. Sight and hearing are neither in the optic nor in the auditory nerves. These organs are the result of man's beliefs that he can see and hear. As his seeing and hearing become finer and truer the organs will reflect the ideas by a more refined appearance than they at present possess. As the body and its organs refine, the chemistry changes and one finds himself in the listening field of life. If we have courage to stand in faith carrying our burdens, we will be given a great force of creative power and in the wake of this wonderful power comes a healing and we open through our auric viewing new vistas of consciousness and we gain auric vision.

Love reveals the innate gifts which make us differ one from another in expression, as one star differs from another in glory. Through love we become dynamos of creative power. Through this discerning power of color we find within us springs of living vibratory chords of music that from the invisible are recorded upon the harp of our souls. It is hard to smile with a singing faith when the heart is being clutched at and we cannot see our way clearly. Obey your inner voice, go your way step by step. Now is your time of testing. You are within the vortex of color and it is receptive to the creative power. Through your channel many truths will be given. So faith must live in you and bring you the answers you have need of. Light will come pouring through wisdom to know your way.

* * *

All that you are you make yourself. I can share with your life and show you the path because I have gone over the path many times and I know its dangers. On this eternal quest we are completely without chart or compass unless some way-shower takes us by the hand and says, "Walk with me." Usually we arrive at the foot of the Mount of Renunciation about the Eighth Plane and from then on endeavor to keep the laws of the Eightfold Path. If we keep those laws we find ourselves very humble for we can always see our faults and know the remedy. Then we are at the gate of the lighted path. You travel on it lighted by God's love. The loom on which you weave your plans is directed from above. The Channel true will be revealed to you. As in silence you wait and seek to see the form of an invisible one and hear the voice softly speak, direction will come when needed to change life's careless ways. The Channel holds and softens your crude thoughtless rays that takes the rainbow from your skies and makes for gloomy days.

* * *

Have faith that from today nothing can keep you from demonstrating in color what you at night have been priviledged to experience. Each man, as he lifts his voice to God, goes into the awful vault of himself. There, alone, he finds truth and if he comes through the door of understanding he finds a way-shower to lead him on. You are on your way. <u>Think color</u>.

* * *

Through understanding one is enlightened and then one has the creative power to heal. We come into the auric color work and lose our false beliefs through color and its creative power. If we love, we have the ability to heal and true healing in color is never an effort. It is the spontaneous love of which we are conscious in the lighted passage through the channel to the presence of our source of supply, our God. We discover ourselves and as individuals know why we are here and quickly realize Christ's promises. For color and beauty is for all.

* * *

No beauty ever comes to us that was not first a vision. Expand the vision, enlarge the ideals through spiritual color and the music that stirs in our hearts. The colors that are born into consciousness will cause us to pause and to realize that the vision of faith is upon us. We have by specific invitation asked faith to abide within the Lighted Path that leads to the channel of our beholding. Our limitations are now passing away and we are seeing through the eyes of the soul. We find great joy in our hearts and we become sharers of another's burdens. Our own we no longer carry. Every auric viewing is a communion in Color.

Faith is based on what is seen — a spiritual experience is the recompense which is never lacking if we keep the sustained contact with God, through the channel. Faith is an insight into the mind of the Creator. A real experience is one in which we are conscious of God's love and power. To grow each day we must expand our region of faith to our reaches of Divine Imagination. Faith is conviction so strong that the results are shown in the rays of the aura called permanent rays.

* * *

Color is an advantage because we need not speak of a special color in our attempt to share it with another. We hold a color in mind when someone is complaining and in faith and humility we are given the proof. Remember human emotions are surface emotions.

* * *

We cannot explain to you nor do we know how the earth feelings of fear, pride, folly, anger, want are changed into faith, love, wisdom, peace and plenty anymore than we know how the soil is changed into the plant, into the animal and all three into man. "The mysterious quickening process" by which the spiritual self changes the natural self into its own likeness is indeed inward, silent, hidden "and we only know of it by the comparison of successive states." One gradually changes in feelings, in character and in conduct. We surrender our earth self by the use of creative power in the channel and a desire to know the divine Self. Transmutation of our heavy emotions are remolded through the color channel.

* * *

My mind has been with you quite often lately. What are you doing with color? Has the course given you a foundation of knowledge that you feel you can share? I will define sight for you as we develop it in the creative silence of the Channel. It is the most bewildering and complex of any of our senses. It is the final and most baffling illusion of the "not self," deepest of all natural errors, demanding for its transmutation the finest and highest Intelligence of reason and will enabled by the Grace of God to work in the right way. For reason and will and all the inner or psychic differentiations of intellect, emotion and volition grouped under such names as mind, heart, soul consciousness are also in their ultimate analysis variations of feeling and the many forms in which feelings are expressed are equally important, so we realize the five senses and every reaction to them must be born in love if we are to know Christ. Therefore beware of merely thinking the meditation. Feel it to the marrow of your bones . . . Learn to be aware of the feeling of the Channel and see only the fairest sights and the sweetest sounds. This is a stiff lesson but if used in the creative silence is a great force in your development.

* * *

You seem a natural for the work. Your personal response to color is geared to your awareness. Unhappy conditions will cause an aversion to certain places, individuals and colors. You can enter a strange home and feel completely at home because of your natural expression in color. To become refreshed, optimistic green is your color. For a calm detached attitude use gray. Gray is an in between color, the color of space between the physical and the real, the waiting color of anticipation without impatience. There are happy colors and there are angry shades. In their natural state all colors are beautiful and positive but when humanity misses the basic shades chaos often results. You cannot find a spot in your world where there is no color because it is a part of creation.

* * *

If we think on colors we are so often charmed by even the sight of color. We teach pure white will draw response from your inner self, overwhelming with light the darkness of any unbalanced emotions. There are happy colors and there are angry shades. In their pure natural state all are beautiful and positive, but when emotion mixes the basic shades chaos often results. Only happy well-adjusted individuals should attempt to initiate God's pure tones. For individual expression can not be left out of anything, no matter how automatic the activity seems to be. In studying and viewing the auric channel the mystical becomes reality. Your understanding as it grows will encounter and absorb shades beautiful beyond those of the mortal plane. The beauty is due to your own awakening, the development of your ability to see with clearer vision. You cannot find a spot in your world where there is no color because it is a part of creation. You contain colors and they contain you. When you can accept, then understand what that means you will really love and make use of the Auric Channel colors.

* * *

To one who lives with understanding in color, there is illumination. And to those who have experienced it there follows a time of receiving visions in the auric channel viewing, and after sufficient development I have had many pupils who have been given cosmic consciousness. In each case the personality changed and then seemed to walk in joy, so uplifted were they. They added two elements to their intellect — a point of view was changed to <u>Universal desire</u> that all man might be given enlightenment; then also a new faculty was added: they had insight in balance.

* * *

Your colors are indeed inspired. I think in these colors we find reverence as if the surface characteristics of life had found a balance in your conscious mind and now you are thinking in all three bodies. These colors are warmed with awareness and courtesy. This course in color you are giving your time to is increasingly charged with spiritual magnetism. The highest results yet known of spiritual development can be yours if you have faith to follow the Rainbow — God's promise to mankind. For those who are in accord with this development of the channel it can be a most fortunate and beautiful experience, a most satisfying response when having asked the Father to open the door between the visible and the invisible, an image intently held in the spiritual and photographed to the physical eye and one sees and knows.

* * *

There are three great tools with which we must work daily. They are prayer, love and joy. Love should be the essence of being since all beings live in the atmosphere of Divine Love.

Remember that joy is the first law of life and we must learn that law. Joy is the fundamental praise to God. It is never too late to learn to use it as a tool. Let us speak on color. God is color of course. As you work in and out of the auric channel you will more and more appreciate color, and you will find your response to color. Eventually you will find you have no dislike of any color. And you cannot use God's marvelous shadings for your best advantage if you do not take them for your individual use. Color is a practical guide to development and understanding.

* * *

Color meditation and prayer will bring perfect repose to mind and body if one can have faith. Self-surrender to God our Father is necessary. There will be times of frustration when doubts will arise in the mind about this course in color. Can it be a science? However strong one's intellectual convictions may be, until certain peculiar experiences occur, such as spiritual hearing or seeing, acceptance is difficult. Glimpses of the invisible are necessary to strengthen the mind and make the student persevere. When you enter auric receiving release your imagination from ordinary concepts. Let it take wing in as many varying images of reassurance as will rise to comfort you. The mind will finally grasp the one color you need at the moment and hold it. When you close your eyes and turn to the great silence of the Channel, you know no boundaries and in one joyous instant a vision is given to you.

* * *

The loving power of God controls and regulates our emotions. You now have gained in capacity beyond conception, a great gift — namely, that throughout life it can serve through visions to enlarge the field of creative work. To overcome, stand in the sandals of another and be tested, then act. Thus the soul is poised in perfect peace.

Here is a formula for security. Time for meditation is a great help in relaxation. Cease hunting for the "safety spot" of security. Security is not a passive condition. Security lies in the alert technique behind the elasticity of nature's forces, the technique of aliveness.

Change is the only constant. Look to the improvement of natural forces and their balance. Security lies in the inherited technique of behavior and readiness to think and feel in all directions and to move quickly when needed. The <u>sense</u> of security lies in an ordered life but change is inevitable.

* * *

Life's basic problems can be solved with blues and greens, these with faith, patience, clear thinking, can be used for energizing healing prayer. In using color healing you are the doctor as well as the patient and an awareness of the love of the indwelling Christ is the medicine. Your seeing color has brought balance and a new knowledge to you of your need to be more closely attuned to your spiritual self. This is growth. I think your development in creative energy through the Auric Channel will serve you and many others. You live and thrive in muted colors. Your Channel is a form of reality and that can be compared to a sunrise or sunset. Our Creator, the Artist. The values of subdued colors painted for us. They are quieting but hearing a voice in the channel or seeing a face means going through varied shades of colors and carrying their creative power through the lighted passage, — then the colors you depict here into the channel.

* * *

We must live in order to make color work for us. For this is the Christ Path. The result of color: "I am quickened in my mind, I am manifesting peace and joy. I am lightened in my heart; its rhythm is expectancy. I am walking in light. I have visions of the night life in spirit. Teachings with color expression pour through me. I awake in the morning with the memory of a burst of glory reaching into the unknown. I am gaining in color faith, hope and love. I become a sharer of color through healing prayer."

* * *

These colors (green, yellow, lavender, light blue) are <u>healing rays for mental fatigue and nerve strain</u>. Rose pink should also be used. This life of yours seems to be balancing into an unusual form of participation. You are on the path of development with an attitude of calmness and you have seen times of stress. You have received love in your life. Love is Color. Color is God. The creative color life is yours.

* * *

Your soul seeking for divine imagination and enlightenment will surely find it, for you have faith and as this paper shows you are now working with the power of creative color. This creative power cultivates and develops the understanding which will enable you to enjoy better health. It improves and strengthens the memory. It develops insight which is so rare, the kind which enables one to see the possibilities as well as the difficulties in every situation. This is a change that takes place by viewing of the channel and one finds things becoming easier in everyday life than ever before. You have carried a heavy load, my dear, now share that load with the faith you know.

* * *

Within this training camp of the Color system he is taught how to set up a station that is correctly attuned to that of his great Commander-in-Chief, God. Here with color he is trained to concentrate his army of thoughts. And as color raises the vibrations of his body he becomes a seeker through the power of Creative energy. He develops insight, feels self-respect and quickly sees the best in all men. Mind is creative and operates through the Law of Attraction.

* * *

We do not know how fear, pride, folly, anger want are changed into faith, love, wisdom, peace and wealth any more than we know how the soil is changed into the plant, the plant into the animal and all three into man, the mysterious quickening process by which the spiritual self changes the natural self into its own likeness. It is inward silent and hidden and we only know of it by comparison of successive states. This is given you as a lesson in teaching as our heavier colors are transmuted into the Channel rays, we live in a state of not just closing our eyes and believing. You are making progress. You aspire to the highest and when you once have lived in the Auric path of light; you can indeed teach color and heal with color.

* * *

Color makes a background for every action, sets the scene for every event. It gives emphasis to living. Color causes surroundings to become more than they have been and helps individuals to awaken to what they are or can be. Color is the strength of the grass, the beauty of the plant life, the grandeur of the skies. Color overwhelms with its rainbows, its auroras. It excites with its sunrises and sunsets. Its tranquility is felt at twilight — great awe with color's mighty display of lightening and thunder clouds. Spiritual reality and a greater refining can take place in your life through color. To use its potentials to the fullest make your colors harmonious to your new faiths and attitudes. Always remember God is color.

* * *

You are on the path of unfoldment and you are doing well. You are now asking your eternal self to aid you in the onward march. It will prove itself to you and you will not be disappointed. The great one you have become in this way of development makes you aware of your need of ignoring surface things, and by use of creative power in color constantly feel the love of your being pouring forth to become one with that which created your conscious person. To live in peace and harmony with your world is expressing the Christ Consciousness.

* * *

You cannot know how happy I am to see this paper. Your faith has set you free. Last night in your night work I found you in a chapel on the Sixth Plane, and found you surrounded on all sides by darting points of light which instead of scorching and withering you like a blown leaf in a storm were like a cool and fragrant shower playing about you. Then you were bathed in a rain of delicate rays like sparkling diamonds and topaz. Then a lovely violet light shrouded you in rich hues of a summer sky and the farther you went the deeper and more glowing was the purple about you. I knew then true faith had become centered and you, my pupil, would grow in color.

* * *

I do feel you are unusually aware now of your responses to color and I believe the refining influence of color will in the future bring you great peace and at-one-ment with the universe. This is a solemn instruction I have used many times when my pupils are re-enacting birth out of the old into reality, as you have pictured on your paper. <u>Instruction</u>: You in this center alone can never stay in one place; you either sink down or are uplifted, for when you <u>neglect</u> the pattern of life you have lived in development, you will find your skies darkening and your sense of freedom dwarfed. Your illumination must not be lessened because you are now a night pupil. Faith is the actual touching of Christ Himself.

* * *

The abundant love of Christ is our solace at all times. My admonition is: Be active in silence by use of color, strong in peace. Thy strength in gentleness, rest in the shelter of Christ's wings about you.

* * *

A gracious happy year to you, my dear friend and may this year bring you balance and create in you the power to fill the inner reaches of your soul with love. The understanding heart that naught can disturb but by the tonal value of your song of life you can sing in color, bathe in color for the creative spirit is color and it is sweetness to your bones and flesh and health and may you reign in this holy estate and by listening through the auric channel receive your guidance. We do know this inner life is only revealed by self-denial and the glorification of the light of Christ's wisdom. Wherever you are, through silence you can touch this secret spark which is eternal, a deathless energy. In color, we see His likeness and the invisible becomes visible and true guidance through balanced thinking can create for us a new world.

* * *

Those whose spirits are stirred (touched) by the breath of Holy Spirit go forward even in sleep. I am trying to reveal to you the unfoldment that has been going on during your work in color. I believe you are now awakening to the joyful, thrilling spirit of the quest. This I know, any neophyte who can become aware of emotions which benumb, frustrate or weave a web of worry can, by the use of color, instantly change these emotions into building blocks of useful material. This can be done without effort through faith — each has within himself a great part to play and no one should judge another as small for the power of God, when man takes hold of it, creates a new man and color pours through the Auric Channel revealing man's abundant energy toward the creation of Christ's kingdom on earth.

* * *

You know there is much more to what we are attempting than the training of people to enter the Auric Channel. The key of the course lies in the sensitiveness which develops from practice in viewing and the balancing power, to use what the Auric channel brings forth. Faith finds God and ennobles the spirit to rest in Him, even while the mind keeps working in both mystery and meaning. You have presented Channel colors. All are the spiritual shades of color. To me, you missed purple as I read these colors. I believe shades of deep purple need to be developed in your case and I also believe purple would be healing to your nerves and be of Auric value to you in reaching out to your son. God bless you dear.

* * *

I will recite our litany of descriptive detail in color. The brightening of colors is one of the beads of our generative Rosary. Green, blue, red, yellow — all stand for wonderful qualities of life and effort. And above all ultimate and basic white. These colors remind us that "Life can be beautiful" for ourselves and others. In such beauty is a fraction of a sunrise, the wonder of a new day. Color expresses qualities in life. Interplay of colored forms is another bead of the same rosary. These colors are given with meditation and brought you healing, increasing your faith in Christ, for more optimism given is your color. It has a magnetic current with which to make contact with the higher forces.

* * *

We really know these color communions calling for spiritual aid to train our sight, for Auric Viewing is stepping into reality. As you go in and out of the Auric Channel you become aware that you are pushing aside the heavy blanket of indifference, old habits and weaknesses. You will be refreshed in a new and boundless freedom because of a great sensitivity to instructions and if you will obey them we know that the still small voice of the Channel is there to be heard. Transfiguration is the term employed in describing the mystical union which takes place in the body of the initiate when the essence of his past experiences reflect through his three bodies making it possible for those who have eyes to see the aura about him.

Colors express life qualities. Man's spiritual usefulness increases as he grows into spiritual consciousness. The time comes when he feels the call to reveal to man through his intellect illuminated with the intuition that which he is to be. At times it is unbelievable that there is a serenity guiding you, healing you. Always the Auric Channel is the Divine Path within and God is color.

* * *

Let us for a moment step back into this holy, immaterial, deathless, timeless quietness of the Auric Channel and consider the vortex of creative power that can be ours if by faith we can commune with the invisible. All during your times of stress or happiness never forget your aura is the sum total of your thought forces and emotions. Your use of sea foam color should aid you as I found it as one of your developing rays. This in the aura denotes true greatness and worthiness.

* * *

Everything has a pulse beat and rhythm. Your response to this color rhythm of the Channel brings awareness of the great harmony of creation. So travel on in released imagination from ordinary concepts. Let it take wing in the Channel with as many varying images of reassurance as will rise to assure. Then your mind will finally grasp the use of color and its application to your every hour of living.

* * *

LIST OF EXCERPTS

Color Used as a Measure of
   True Spirituality 147
Learning to See Color 148
Love Colors: Rose and Cerise 149
The Life of Faith in Color 149
Patience and the Channel 150
Creative Color Channel 152
Using the Channel 152
Self-Mastery 153
Personal Responsibility 153
Prayer 154
Prayer, a Power for Change 154
Courtesy 155
The Spirit of Criticism 156
The Great One You Are 157
Patience and Other Principles 157
Two Parallel Modes 158
Psychological Findings and
   Color Therapy 159
Finding Your Own Reality 160
Peace 161
Soul Expression Through Color 163
Repose 163
Power 164
Vibration 165
Aura 165
Teaching by Mary 166
The Heavenly Way 167

Chapter 6

EXCERPTS — PERTINENT WRITINGS

> The Heavenly Way is a Mystic Way
> And the Mystic Way seems a strange way.
>   Mary D. Weddell

The following are excerpted from the writings of Mary D. Weddell, George W. Weddell, M.D., and Miriam B. Willis. Authorship is indicated by the initials M.D.W., G.W.W. and M.B.W., respectively. The few unsigned articles were written by Mary or Dr. George Weddell, or by both together.

COLOR USED AS A MEASURE OF TRUE SPIRITUALITY

Color and the Channel were given to me to challenge me and cause me to worship God more reverently. The Color brought me knowledge of serenity. The Channel brought me balance in thinking, patience in waiting for belief to develop into faith's unique security.

If one becomes a seeker he accepts the fact that his life is strictly between himself and God. Color helps the seeker to discipline his speech, that he may seek clarity rather than cleverness and sincerity instead of sarcasm. The seeker knows that disciplined thinking and action gives him wisdom and grace to accept life's pattern as traced upon his soul at birth. He realizes these patterns will be given him again through dreams, visions and the revelations received in his night work on higher planes.

The proof of man's development is private, personal, intimate, spiritual beyond the compass of speech, too sacred, too vast, too fragile to be poured into the cold, unsympathetic molds of human language. Development of spiritual power through the Color Channel is an intuitive gift that causes one to burst forth in the rapture of faith and to listen for the whispers of love and promise of eternal life. Always remember illumination must come from within.
                                                                                         —M.D.W.

LEARNING TO SEE COLOR

One Way of Visual Sensitivity Training

We can open our eyes to the vibrations of color, concentrating with a lighted candle or lamp, (but never at the sun). We first look intently at the light and then close our eyes and look at the interior field of vision, straight ahead, apparently through the eyelids. A field of darkness will appear, which after a few moments is differentiated into colors. As one continues looking, this color will become a wave of light or localize into a distinct spot. This spot will be large or small, according to the intensity of the concentration. In those who are color blind, the spot will be indefinite in form for some time. With those who are active in color sight, both objectively and subjectively, the waves of light or spot will form instantly, remain for a long time, and be extremely well defined.

The old-thought individual will often say, "Oh I can get all that color by just pressing my eyeballs." — True he can, and this is proof positive to the skeptical mind that this higher vibratory law of vision exists, but he never stops to think of the pathos of a state of consciousness which has to press its eyeballs or look at a light or do some physical thing to awaken within himself a law of being which the developed mind uses as the natural accompaniment of its daily life. When we have developed our subjective vision, we do at will what the undeveloped life can only do by operating physical means.

When one presses on his eyeballs, he excites the hyper-activity of the visual centers and brings into play the forces which are latent in these centers but active in the developed eye. A person should practice with lights, candles, electrical apparatus, etc., until he has awakened his full visual activity, then it will not be long before the color vision becomes the natural accompaniment of sight.

After one has become familiar with the auric colors and by these induced states of vision has fully expressed his power to see, the next thing is to know and understand what he sees.

Place yourself in a comfortable position and then gaze directly and intensely at a light. After a few moments, close your eyes and try to find the color in your subjective vision. Repeat until you can see the light with your eyes closed, then find the color with your eyes open. When you have succeeded in this attempt, then you are ready to go on. Look at the light, and when thoroughly at one with all the colors, begin the inbreathing of long deep breaths, putting into your mind and into the light the thought of the color you desire to vibrate. As you go on watching the flame, you will begin to see around it a white light. This is the highest play of vibratory ether, and as you continue to look you will see the intensified rays of color.

All the colors which appear in the light are the different vibrations of sense which are active in you. If you wish to know your auric colors, you know them by watching these shades.

Should any form, faces, landscapes or flowers or any other objects appear in the light, it is the effort of your mind to express the thought in your aura. Most of these things are thought forms. The brain receives pictures after the fashion of a camera producing negatives.

When a student commences to vibrate to this visual extension, all previous impressions of faces, thoughts and objects which have been impressed on his brain begin to develop and become manifest before him. This is often misleading, for students fancy they are psychic faces and forms. Sometimes a person really gets the second extension of vision and sees psychically, but not in his first attempts. One who has true psychic vision is not dependent on light or material aids — he simply sees.

When you have practiced this light concentration long enough the white light will remain, and color, pictures — everything — disappear. Then you can know that you are conquering physical sense and emotion and are coming into a subjective state where you can place into this white light whatever you desire to see developed, and you can stop at any vibration and function normally; you can induce any state of thought and feeling you desire, see any color and hear any keynote.

This training gives the student the power to stay his reflections — and leads him farther and farther on to universal wisdom. He will learn to extend his vision and hearing until he can encompass even the third and fourth dimensions of space.

—G.W.W.

LOVE COLORS: ROSE AND CERISE

Rose is the human love color. As your vibrations are raised into more delicate tints of soft red and pink tints the love vibration is lifted above the personal plane. Love is always love, but it has many degrees of unfoldment and different states of consciousness, and it brings forth health, strength and vitality. The rosy tints are of the greatest importance because they are the highest vibration of the evidence of God's Love in action. The addition of rose — some yellow — and pink is the evidence of Universal Creative Consciousness in action.

—M.D.W.

THE LIFE OF FAITH IN COLOR

The use of color in our lives is a means of development over a God-given path of intelligent safety.

As with a flame, we may light a wick, and the color of the flame of the burning wick will depend on the nature of the wick and the liquid in which it is soaked. So in each human being there is the light of God's love. If it becomes a flame, man is on the path of development, and the flame will readily inform the reader of auras whether he has overcome his ego, and to what degree he is in control of his emotional desire-body. The colors, as they are used, set in motion by the spiritual desire-body, prove balanced thinking has aided in the development of spiritual enlightenment. He is now living by spiritual principles, sincerely longing to have his intuitions as a guide, and knowing experience to be the only means to open the eyes of the intelligence, aware also that careful self-training is necessary ere he can recognize a voice out of the great silence speaking to him.

May the purple robe of faith envelop you in your daily needs.

—M.D.W.

PATIENCE AND THE CHANNEL

In order to grow spiritually one needs great patience, and this patience is the happy fruit of discipline. It is that quality which gives a glow to the discipline of waiting, and I will turn now with you to that beautiful colored channel within the being of each one of you, the pathway of light that glows with the energy of the soul.

Above Faith is the Holding Force of Patience. Beloved, it takes, oft-times, a great endurance of patience to hold your faith. Faith is such an invisible and ephemeral quality, yet you have proven in your lives over and over again that faith is the power of God functioning through humanity when that humanity is relying on God's power. Yes, it is the Royal Purple of Faith, and you mount from that premise to the Holding Force of Patience.

What do you hold through patience? You hold back the sudden impulses, the quick desires, the unpremeditated impulse that may run you into difficulty, the prideful opinion that lacks tolerance. Those are the things, and many more, that require that silver lavender of patience. Any why is the silver? It is the influence of the Christ Spirit.

And now step up the Pink Lavender of Inspiration. Can you fulfill inspiration without patience? Can you develop any harmonious, beautiful thing without patience? Patience is the bulwark against the overflow, or flooding, that guards each of these steps that you climb. For the fulfillment of the inspiration in all its delicate color rays, its swift traveling through your being, you require patience to perfect the inspiration, to bring it into creation. I give you that to think on.

And now mount with me to the Rose Lavender of the Spiritual Voice. How can you hear the spiritual voice without patience? How do you attain the greater growth in the quality of that spiritual voice without patience? Does it ever cut across that which you thought you were going to do, that which you had impulsively already done? Does it ever require a blind trust to obey that spiritual voice within you? And if you refuse to obey time and time again and follow your own impulse, does it grow? Or do you dull that voice of your own conscience, the Christ voice within you?

You alone can answer these questions for yourselves. I give you the gift of patience. Use this silver lavender and you will stumble less, and you will fulfill the rose lavender of the listening to the inner voice. It is the gift to every man, the light of his conscience.

Now climb with me to the Blue Orchid of Prophecy. Do you listen when you are uncertain whether you should go this way or that? Do you draw that color to you to give you the clear answer of direction before the deed is performed, before it is born into your action or into the words of your voice or the power of your thinking? Those are all parts of those beautiful color rays that have been given to you for your using; that must be developed by you through your using. And the Holding Force of Patience keeps you steady and harmoniously where you should be.

Now step with me over the Yellow Bridge of Enlightenment that lifts us to the Rose Orchid of the Message Bearer. What message is worthwhile if you do not listen to the inner voice of guided direction? How many times in your life have you already, through the mercy and power and influence of the spirit, avoided the wrong direction or been able to give the right direction to yourself or someone else? You are, and everyone is, a message bearer by your very life. Is it an impatient life? An impulsive life? An unsteady life that is out of balance? How are you going to bring it into the fruition of the harmonious law of rightful vibratory action within your being without patience?

Patience never wears out. It's ofttimes the backward-forward movement for the larger embrace of a holding force. All these things are included in that silver lavender.

And now we mount to the Red Lilac of the Holding Force for the Band of Teachers. Give us this color when you meet in circle. Give us that powerful ray to stand upon. You desire to develop the power to give the message. Hold these rays of harmonious color within your being and trust — which is another facet of patience, a holding power of assurance. Hold it quietly that you may give the foundation of stability to our higher forces, that you may hear the message that we bring.

Now we need a step upward in the cycle of enlightenment to the very core of your being, within your being, the Glowing Peach of Union of Mind and Spirit. Bear it to whom you give your mind. What servant do you want your mind to be? Do you want it to be the instrument of the Most High? Is it your promised treasure if you use and apply the color rays to the maturity of your fruit within you? You know that it is, and we know that it is, so draw within your being this glowing peach of Union of Mind and Spirit. Let patience keep it steady. Let patience keep it balanced. Let patience bring through this balance and this steadiness, the maturity of the voice, the voice of wisdom, the voice of love, the voice of selfless utter caring for anyone who needs the gift that you have.

This must lead to Brotherhood, that Blue Orchid, the light, light blue orchid that is ever infiltrated with the lightest blue to bring this to the good earth, and now the New Age may cause it to be the norm of life on this planet — the brother that would lay down his life for another. Do you need patience when your brother is slandering you or critical of you? When you see that he is going the wrong way, what do you need? Do you need a flash of temper to match his own or do you need patience? Do you need to let patience have her perfect work that Christ triumph within you?

And does it seem natural to you, as I talk to you, my dear friends, that this brotherhood would lead thee to the serenity of peace in your soul? The soul is no longer agitated when brotherhood is fulfilled. The soul then functions in Serenity, that Blush Orchid ray that is so high and so real and so powerful. So powerful that you are lifted out of your self-desire into the universal desire of the light, light pale green bridge and into the Rose Bisque of Grace, the benediction of His "Well done".

Isn't that great? The benediction of the Voice saying in the soul, "Well done." You let the spirit of God speak through you. You hold the fort through the Holding Force of Patience, and this brings Peace, that strong fortress of the Light Blue Lavender that holds its quiet when the tongue wants to fly off. No wonder it's close to the color of patience, for you cannot have peace without patience. And yet if you love patience you will have peace even at the end of a stormy day. It may be you will have as you say in your vernacular, what is it? "Kept your cool." You have held the fort. You have been endowed with the blessed praise of patience developed into peace.

And here the door of your inner being is open to the inflow and the outflow of the oneness of the two worlds, the spirit functioning through the human vehicle, through the human channel. Beloved, treasure the power of patience to develop and bring your life into flowering and into fruition that others may eat and drink of the fruit of your being and be blessed with brotherhood.

God bless you, my beloved students, God bless you.

From a high spirit guide of Color
Through —M.B.W.

CREATIVE COLOR CHANNEL

Along the Path of development the seeker arrives at a mesa of Universal Consciousness. As he observes the sign posts he reads "This Way Alone." At this point great stress is laid on outer conditions. The mastery of pride, the control of appetites and desires are the first important steps, and one needs guidance for he must depend upon his intellect. His mind can lead him into many bypaths, for appearances are deceiving. Sometimes a man at this stage seems insincere and vascillating. Eventually, through trial and error and the love of the Universal Path, man is once again the seeker. Then his intellectual supremacy wanes while soul-consciousness assumes domination. This is the first high point along the way. Symbol of the second stage he is given through Creative Color a vision nourished in the heart, and begins the assimilation of spiritual truth and the illuminated power to use his intuitions in the conquest of his emotional nature.

There are no psychic limitations to inner vision. The psychic faculties of man know no barriers of space or time. A world of marvelous phenomena awaits your command. Within the natural but unused functions of your mind are dormant powers which can bring about a transformation of your life.

USING THE CHANNEL

As you climb the spiralled channel of your inner being and reach its summit, you free your soul to consciously breathe the pure air of the higher order and open the door of heaven, receiving more fully the rhythm of the spheres that sets the pace for your communication throughout your day. Hold this treasured experience and let it guide and bless you, thus adding to your permanent growth. Nothing can flavor each endeavor with a better seasoning. Nothing satisfies the hunger more than replenishment of loving power that descends and nurtures. It is a consciousness to be renewed by climbing this mount several times during the day and leaves its blessing just before sleep frees the soul for each night's adventure. It is the guardian of the soul and builds protection of the higher way, the lighted path of spiritual attainment, into natural growth — gentle, loving and strong.

—M.D.W.

SELF-MASTERY

In your search for self-mastery we find that you need not relinquish anything of value in order to recognize your own divine spirit. In Sanskrit the word "man" means the power to think. There are no material physical steps by which to reach this awareness of your real self. This is accomplished by your power to think. You were created in the image of God. Your central intelligence which does not die, which does not pause in any dimension at any time, can direct your physical intelligence, your mind, so you can win the struggle which goes on constantly in your brain.

The human mind, as you know, is a willful thing. If it is worthwhile to you to lose all of the unhappiness you have known and to find all of the joy you have longed for, then turn your life over to that great Creative Intelligence and let it be your guide. Direction will come and your awareness, your growth is up to you.

The search for understanding is a long and dreary way to the stubborn, the proud and the willful ones. There is no long journey to take unless the mind wishes it to be long, no high mountains to climb — the human ego has built such things. We erect our own barrier between God and ourselves.

Your color channel makes a background for your development. For every action color sets the scene, for every event it gives emphasis to living and helps individuals to awaken to what they are. Color, the grandeur of the skies, it is one more feelable proof of God. Everyone who reaches the awareness hears the music of the spheres, and in the sound itself the adoration for God is fully expressed.

—M.D.W.

PERSONAL RESPONSIBILITY

How many men and women today carry the burdens of their personal responsibilities in such a manner as to obtain therefrom the highest degree of constructive spiritual development and the fullest measure of psychic unfoldment of which they are capable?

The largest measure of benefit to every student who receives this training comes to him as a result of the personal effort he puts forth in the solution of his problems. Among our individual acquaintances, each one of us will be able to recall one or more who have deeply impressed us with a sense of their melancholy martyrdom to duty. Many of our friends show to some extent that they are burdened with more than their share of responsibilities which causes unhappiness and misery.

What a rude awakening awaits all those who measure life from this erroneous viewpoint. A life filled with such frustrating thoughts is reaping a harvest of tares, and cannot gain spiritual enlightenment.

First, self-respect must be gained by accepting our personal responsibilities. Also, one must feel the impulse to change the attitude toward life, endeavoring to give back to life and God what has continually been given.

The higher view of this one supreme and inalienable right of individual existence is that life itself is of no value, either to the individual or to the world, except insofar as it has gained development and served God and humanity.

PRAYER

Great Father to whom we are all but children, Friend of the friendless and Helper of those who need be our friend when other friends have failed us, be our Helper in the hour of our extremity.

Great Father, insofar as may be for our mutual good, be with us this day and through all the days of our earthly life. Lead us by the hand of love. Point us to the pathway of duty, Great Father. Bear with us when we stumble over the pathway which leads onward and upward into Light. We shall hope one day to stand with You in the midst of the radiant splendor of eternal truth. We shall be ever grateful. Amen.

—G.W.W.

PRAYER, A POWER FOR CHANGE

Prayer has a great power in the development of mankind. Prayer removes mental strain, and ofttimes one sending out prayer on Color will find the one prayed for subconsciously received a beneficial response. Prayer is an upliftment. It does not banish disease, but it takes away some of the sickening emotions that follow on the heavy vibration of a sick body.

The union of the two worlds can be realized by the opening of the Auric Channel and seeing with the spiritual eye clearly into the Higher Planes. Every day as you go forth, think of those higher realms of activity that are just beyond the reach of man's consciousness. If you could for one hour each day spend time in the Channel colors, a great deal that is flowing at an uneven force in your body would be cleared and a more healthful ray would be given you. If you do truly desire the rightness of things first be right with yourself and expect of no man what you do not want to give.

Please remember, development requires an illumining mind that awakens to the forces about you, and when one is awakened, one becomes aware and alerted to growth. Emotions stop progress. Here the use of Color proves its value.

The discontented mind can be the greatest drawback in the use of Color plumes. So often these minds of ours float out into space, taking in so many things we can scarcely comprehend the law of development when we meet up with it. So let us conserve our spiritual energies and open our eyes and see the area of power being extended to us.

—M.D.W.

COURTESY

Courtesy is the perfume of life. The most serene sweetness that can emanate from an individual is that essence of personal effacement called courtesy. The pristine beauty of the gesture of always receding that another may accede is truly only the prerogative of the really great.

The spirit from which emanates this rare delicacy of the virtues must be truly one in touch with the divine. An unconscious movement to allow another to take precedence can only arise from the soul that has transcended the small and petty things of life.

In the consciousness of the truly courteous is the fundamental knowledge of the inherent greatness of all of God's creation. The fusion sense that transcends selfishness is the mainspring of action where a manifestation of courtesy abounds.

The great Master said, "He who would be greatest among you must be the servant of all." No greater law was ever given than the one that says "All life is one and emanates from God." Hence, the sense of granting obeisance to all of God's creation is the external evidence of the truly gifted and developed soul.

Courtesy is the greatest diplomat the world has ever known. No one can succeed in an undertaking if his manners are crude and offensive. So in the realm of mundane things the higher law works itself out, showing that all life here and hereafter is from a common source and has a common purpose.

The sense of separateness which in its last analysis is the only sin possible for man to commit is always in evidence where courtesy is absent. The truly courteous sees the reflection of God in all His creatures and his respect is the unconscious reverence he has for the Creator. The handiwork of God is and always will be worthy of the reverence that any of us can bestow on it. So the unfailing courtesy that is given in all places is the outcropping of the spirit of reverence inherent in the individual.

The courtesy granted woman in the general scheme of life is a recognition of her close relationship to the Divine and her great sense of proportion of the true value of the spirit of life. Will she in her high spiritual forces and intuitions find herself remiss in the new day where chivalry and courtesy are mocked by her sex? This is truly the greatest sign of degeneration of the age.

To know true courtesy we must become aware of the Law of Cause and Effect or balance. If one fears God he cannot get past that fear. Give God your unquestioning trust and you will consciously receive His constant protection.

You are on the threshhold of unfoldment, for truth is close and of easy access. Through awareness, at any instant you might get a glimpse into the realms now unseen. This is every soul's adventure if so desired and when he can feel that love which is carried upon the magnetic current throughout the atmosphere, courtesy and consideration are a part of his surface self.

So courtesy has its origin in the deference accorded our fellowman. Let us make courtesy our watchword for on its fair fields of endeavor grow the sweetest and most beautiful flowers that never fade and whose brilliancy leads us into the splendor of divine truth.

—G.W.W.

THE SPIRIT OF CRITICISM

The most destructive and disintegrating factor that can creep into any organization is the spirit of criticism. This hydra-headed monster is the keystone of the arch of discord, upon which the powers of darkness depend to destroy all constructive movements. Preying upon the principle elements of the personality, they too often succeed.

Let us analyze the fundamentals of this ill-visaged effect. Primarily its taproot is vanity. Vanity not so much of person as of opinion. An inordinate desire to appear important and intellectual, in comparison to the one criticized. It partakes of the various elements of boastfulness, obtrusive personality, conceit, self-esteem, pretension, self-approbation.

How little we are aware when we criticize another that we are attempting to recommend ourselves for the position occupied by the envied one. What might appear to us as just disagreement soon follows its line of least resistance and evolves into destructive effort, and will find its resting place in ill humor, backbiting and even slanderous remarks.

Our venerable leader has summed up the whole matter in these words, "Walk with me while we can agree, but friendly always when we disagree." Keep the love light burning in your heart for the one who might be in error from your standpoint, and gradually that one will see your point of view without the spoken word. The dark gray clouds that surround one upon whom your critical thoughts are turned will so enervate that normal judgment and mental function is impossible. Instead of helping, you are magnifying the difficulty.

Always remember that the Masters do not criticize, and that the spirit is not theirs, but the powers of darkness ride into your consciousness on these darts of envy and jealousy that objectify in criticism.

Keep your feet fixed on the Rock of Love around which the waves of tolerance continually break, and your soul will be washed clean of that sullen spirit and in its stead rises the Sun of Righteousness and the alabaster form of helpfulness.

Out of the alembic will flow the joy of privilege and each opportunity will be one to grow and evolve. The perfect example was when the Master told the self-righteous Pharisees, "He that is without sin, let him cast the first stone". Do not be a rock thrower, but a rock placer, one who builds, not one who destroys.

—G.W.W.

THE GREAT ONE YOU ARE

The great one you are in reality will answer your every true need and longing, where your conscious mind expresses a living faith. You are on the threshold of unfoldment each time you enter the Channel of Color. At any instant you can take the one short step into the realms of fulfillment.

If you sincerely yearn to know the pure formula of life, the way to express your faith at once; if you humbly look with open, eager mind for understanding that you may be the physical expression God planned you to be, you will receive enlightenment through faith.

You, like all other expressions of God, will inevitably reach the goal of development and awareness. Inevitably, you will come to a place on your pathway where the signpost is clearly marked for your mind. It reads, "Alone from this point on."

First, you must be aware of the closeness of God to your conscious being, that it may express unwavering faith. Then, you will understand the laws of Creation, and realize you are truly loved.

Bless you. May awareness, faith and understanding be yours forever.

—M.D.W.

PATIENCE AND OTHER PRINCIPLES

It is never easy for any of us to hold onto principles, convictions and ideals. Something sinister in the nature of things is always seeking to take them away from us and make us cynics. But when we are strong enough to hold fast, even in the midst of tragedy and disaster, we will invariably find new strength for ourselves, and often a blessing for others, too.

We all lose our patience now and then. Many people are inclined to believe that it does us good to "blow off steam" once in a while. One can be certain, in development, that one pays a high price by losing one's temper and wounding another. He then realizes he has lost self-mastery, and his record of self-control has once more torn down his wall of defenses.

I often see in this skeptical world many people overcoming fear and guilt. In this way miracles can still occur — when men _act_ their faith as well as preach it. And love gets a chance to show its power.

Sometimes you hear a person say, "I never really make an impression. I feel unwanted." The definition of shyness as given by a noted psychoneurologist: Shyness is paralysis that comes from an exaggerated sense of our own importance. Are you afraid you will not be welcomed? Afraid you will not hold your own in conversation? Remember you are thinking that, and anyone can gain self-respect and friends if he pays the price. The price is high in the beginning but yields great profits.

TWO PARALLEL MODES

The Conscious and the Subconscious Mind

The operations of the mind are produced by two parallel modes of activity, the one conscious and the other subconscious. Conscious mind is reasoning will. Subconscious mind is instinctive desire, the result of past reasoning will.

The subconscious mind draws just and accurate inferences from premises furnished from outside sources. When the premise is true the subconscious reaches a faultless conclusion, but where the premise or suggestion is in error, the whole structure falls. The subconscious does not engage in the process of proving. It relies upon the conscious mind, the "Watchman at the Gate", to guard it from mistaken impressions. The conscious mind ought to be on duty every waking hour, for when the "Watchman" is off guard or when its calm judgment is suspended, the subconscious mind is left open to suggestions from all sources.

The conscious mind has the facility of discrimination, the power of reasoning. It is the seat of the will and may impress the subconscious which is instinctive desire. Thought is a creative energy and will automatically correlate with its object and bring it into manifestation. If, therefore, the subconscious desire is in harmony with the forward movement of the great whole, creative forces will be set in motion which will bring about the result of the operation of the Law of Attraction.

When the "Watchman" opens the gate to the inflow of spirit, heavy impurities, lethargies and ignorance are burned away, creating spiritual growth. The beginning of spiritual health, understanding and creative energy are gifts that will make you free, for they will guide you to stand within your inner now and look out undismayed through the outer you, thus changing your basic plan of life to become more alive and aware of this inward growth instead of going through life to be tempered. As a seeker you deliberately illumine yourself with this creative energy that gets your feet upon the "Lighted Path" of soul development.

The endowment of the five senses are the gateways of man's inner and outer being through which he communicates with the world outside and the world within. If he sees or hears something sad his sympathy is touched; if he sees or hears something tragic he is shocked. Music, beauty, gaiety and laughter create an uplifting reaction of joy, gladness, etc. Through his memory and imagination he can picture a myriad of things his eyes and ears have seen and heard. This phenomenon is so natural that he ceases to marvel. Hence, we realize that here are sensing faculties within as well and through these, intuitive flashes register in the mind. We believe that man has come to this earth school to further develop his spiritual being and that he is endowed with the necessary potential to develop his spiritual senses of sight, hearing, touch, etc. Sensing is often the beginning of this development in intuitive knowing.

As the Master said, "If thine eye be single thy whole body will be full of Light."

PSYCHOLOGICAL FINDINGS AND COLOR THERAPY

Consider that because there is action and interaction throughout the whole of life, this process between the conscious and subconscious requires a similar action in the corresponding system of nerves. The Cerebro-Spinal System is the organ of the conscious mind and the Sympathetic System is the organ of the subconscious mind. The Cerebro-Spinal is the channel through which we receive conscious perception from the physical senses and exercise control over the movements of the body. This system of nerves has its center in the brain.

The Sympathetic System has its center in a ganglionic mass at the back of the stomach known as the Solar Plexus and is the channel which unconsciously supports the vital functions of the body.

The connection between the two systems is made by the vagus nerve which passes out of the cerebral region as a portion of the voluntary system to the thorax, sending out branches to the heart and lungs, and finally passing through the diaphragm. Here, it becomes identified with the nerves of the Sympathetic System, thus forming a connecting link between the two, making man physically a single entity.

Recall that every thought is received by the brain — the organ of conscious mind, and here subjected to the power of reasoning. When this objective mind accepts the thought it is transmitted to the Solar Plexus — the brain of the subconscious — where it is made flesh — to be brought forth into the world as a reality. It is then no longer susceptible to any argument whatever, for the subconscious mind cannot argue. It only acts. It accepts the conclusions of the objective mind as final.

The Solar Plexus is like the Sun of the body because it is the central point of distribution for the energy which the body is constantly generating.

This is very real energy and is distributed by very real nerves to all parts of the body. It extends in etheric substance, surrounding the body and is known as the "aura" or the orbit in which man lives and moves and has his being. Here, all that he is, is reflected in living color generated from the channel within the Solar Plexus.

When this process is functioning perfectly man is in health and happiness, radiating life, energy and vitality to everyone he meets.

The Solar Plexus is the point at which the part meets the whole, where the finite becomes the infinite, where the uncreate becomes create, where the universal becomes individualized, the invisible becomes visible.

This center of energy is Omnipotent because it is the point of contact with all life and all intelligence.

It can accomplish whatever it is directed to accomplish — and herein lies the power of the conscious mind. The subconscious can and will carry out plans and ideas suggested by the conscious mind.

Conscious thought, then, is master of the Sun Center from which the life energy of the entire body flows, and the quality of thought which we entertain determines the quality of the thought which this sun will radiate, and the character of the thought entertained by our conscious mind determines the thought which this Sun will radiate and consequently will determine the nature and experience which will result.

It is evident that all we have to do is let our Light shine. Feed it with the living substance of Color rays that cleanse and uplift transmuting undesirable thinking into harmonious fulfillment.

Yield to Color in non-resistant thought. It expands the Solar Plexus while resistance contracts. Thoughts of faith, courage, love, confidence and hope all produce a corresponding state.

The one arch enemy of the Solar Plexus is fear. This energy must be completely destroyed by the application of Color, for color has the power to still the busy mind, to calm the undisturbed emotions and to nourish and bring one into a unified whole of expanding consciousness and growth.

—G.W.W.

FINDING YOUR OWN REALITY

Wholeness is a sense sublime of something far more deeply interfused. The term "universe", applied to the existent system of creation, in its significance reveals a great fundamental quality of creation in essential oneness or wholeness.

The most advanced thought in the realms of theology, philosophy and material science tends to confirm the perfect fitness of this choice — a term to designate the full expression of the one life, the one spirit, which informs all, shows all things, and weaves the vari-colored threads of existence into magnificent design.

Every created thing takes its significance from its relationships to other created things and to the whole great plan. All meaning resides in relationship and in relationship only — there is no other meaning. The difference between the little, undisciplined mind and the disciplined mind is found in the fact that the former sees detached things and events, while the latter sees the same things and events in their larger relationships and in logical sequence.

Our life pattern is built in the thought world. Before a pattern is materialized in a life, it is completed in thought. It is pushed into visibility by the forces of the emotional world. The thought pattern is the arrow. The emotion is the bow.

So man creates his life by his secret thoughts. Therefore, as a man thinketh in his heart — through his emotional world — so he is. It follows, then, that any man can know the kind of man he really is by analyzing his innermost thoughts. However, where we make tragedies in our lives is in mistaking thought for truth. Our thoughts and truth may be entirely different things. We must always bear in mind "Truth is truth and will always prevail".

If our thinking is not truth, we must think it all over again.

We must think in the white light of truth. If a man is what he thinketh in his heart, if life's pattern is made in the thought world, then man must not only rethink his life in the blazing white light of truth, but he must start all over again and relive his life in the white light of truth.

Color, correctly applied, establishes truth in the inner man and will manifest in his life. That being the case, the important thing is not in the thinking but in the finding of truth first, and thinking and living from that point. Seek truth!!!

All of us have goals and desires, things we hope to do with our lives, situations we want to manifest and see happen. It is most often the case that in order to achieve any specific thing, we have to be ready for it or have the qualities within ourselves to attract it. All too often our very natures are our worst enemies. Therefore, we have to be willing to look at ourselves and to make an effort to erase our negative traits and those qualities that are holding us back, in order to grow into positive ones. This is exactly what color does for us.

Truth comes to the open-minded. The higher truths you now hold have come to you in direct proportion to your attainment of discipline.

Let us speak for a moment about discipline, a beneficent force which is ultimately revealed as involuntary strength in times of need. Your desire is to be strong and clean enough within through self-discipline to bring to fulfillment the benefits that faithful application of color will give you — Love in action.

Prayer: "Create in me a clean heart, O God,
And renew a right spirit within me."

—M.D.W.

PEACE

Peace be unto thee. I cannot imagine a greeting that is pregnant with as much meaning as "peace be unto thee". You know I doubt if we ever stop to think just what we mean when we say those four words.

Peace is the perfect blending of the entire universe into one harmonious whole, without a single dissenting atom. Peace means a perfect love and a perfect understanding, an abiding light that will shine in all dark places. No sorrow or misunderstanding can abide with peace. No turmoil is so great that this magic word does not turn the whitecaps of trouble into low waves of unrest which are succeeded by a beautiful calm where the weary soul finds rest.

The inner conflict is the one that takes the greatest strength, for that is the part that has some claim to permanency. When the heart can feel the soothing notes of approaching peace and the mind settles into the restful groove of content, then happiness is very near.

The outer conditions are ever fluctuating and changing so no sense of perfect peace is possible where there is so much impermanency. Can you imagine that autos or houses can bring peace? Can you see any happiness connected with money except as it is used as a trust and spent for the help and comfort of others? Is there anything that so ruins and debauches like that self-same money? Yet withal it is one of the greatest blessings given to man, for with it great joy and peace can be given. Peace seldom is associated with it not because of it, but because of our hearts concerning it.

Harmony is peace, peace is love, love is life and life is eternal. Think on these things, meditate on them in your heart. No one is at peace who has a single urge within his consciousness to work or think against another. The very stress of that builds up a great wall that forever and effectively shuts out the very thing desired.

So if we want peace we must think first of the comfort and happiness of our fellowman and in the urgent seeking we will find the Holy Grail that has so far eluded us.

The angry waves that surge and roar on the bleak and rockbound coasts are not criterions of contentment. They represent the ultimate of opposition and the summit of discontent. But even they can be stilled by the filmy layer of oil that prevents contact of the opposing forces. So you can often be the emissary of peace, the oil that quells and subdues. Nations spring at each others throats at the smallest trifles largely because some national vanity has been offended. These things are so small in God's great universe that they scarcely cause a ripple in the cosmos, yet they create great sorrow and suffering.

No great reward having a claim to permanency has ever been the sequel of contention. Business builded on the principle of cooperation always has at least as much again to hold it as one builded on competition. The competitive strain weakens the moral fiber and nullifies the effort. It is the boll weevil of business structure, for upon it rests the blame of all business failure. Peace as a watchword, cooperation as a banner and loving kindness as a beacon light will pilot many a sinking barque to a shore of safety.

The inward peace of heart and mind is the open sesame to bodily health and comfort. No mind dwelling on the mutable conditions of material things, blinding itself to the eternal verities of spirit can ever — can ever — remain in a vehicle of comfort. Water and oil will not mix, hence the great divergence of permanency and impermanency, as manifested in matter and spirit will never find a common ground of action.

We sink into a despond when the natural mutations of the substance of material shows unusual activity, because we are fixed in our determination to anchor our affections to the reactions of the senses. To be happy we must transcend the mutations and see the cosmic urge that centers itself in the higher vehicles. Mind far transcends matter, and it only requires a little thought to realize the effects produced by mental states. The inward peace of mind characteristic of the truly great, creates a greater stability of conditions than prevails in the hasty erratic efforts of those who have no fixed purpose and poise that stands these changes.

—G.W.W.

Bellevue, Washington

February 1, 1927

(Taken from a personal letter of Dr. Weddell's to a friend.)

SOUL EXPRESSION THROUGH COLOR

Were I called upon to define, very briefly, the term "Color", I should call it the reproduction of what the senses perceive in nature through the veil of the soul. No one can explain how the notes of a Mozart melody or the folds of a piece of Titian's drapery produce their essential effects. If you do not feel it, no one can by reasoning make you feel it.

A work of art in color is a corner of creation seen through a temperament.

It is the treating of the commonplace with the feeling of the sublime that gives to art its true power.

Art is a human activity consisting in this, that one man consciously, by means of certain external signs, hands on to others feelings he has lived through and that other people are infected by these feelings and also experience them.

—M.D.W.

REPOSE

The calm of eventide calls all to rest and quietude. When the setting sun tolls the knell of parting day all life and action should take its cue and seek the quiet of departing day, and be content to be enfolded in the sable cloak of night and to lie down to peaceful sleep. The rhythm of life calls us to repose when the shades of night fall around us, and here is the time to seek communion with our inner spirit and contact that Divine Vibration wherein only can we find perfect peace.

Continued turmoil and physical action completely inhibits contact with the hidden forces resident in the realms of Being. Hence, at the time of repose, the soul finds its flight to higher planes unimpeded. All turmoil is of the body and not of the Spirit. The overpowering influence of the sense perceptions leads us into the error that Reality consists of much going to and fro in the world of materiality, but it is only an illusion for the quieting of the senses and the consequent opening of the supernal break into the opening soul, and the radiant light of Spirit erases all sense perceptions.

This is entering the Silence, opening the superconsciousness, transcending the illusion of matter, or seeing the Unseen. This glorious consummation of effort is only compatible with Repose. The words of real life are written on the scroll of the Hidden or Unseen, and the key for their solution lies in the soul consciousness which is ever buried in the rubbish of the Temple, and the cleansing process must be instituted ere the neophyte is able to penetrate the glories of illumination. Repose is the watchword of the neophyte who expects to surmount the hills of Selfishness and Sensation.

How true it was when the Great Master gave the occult law: "He who would find his life must first lose it." This has been a hidden, obscure expression of this law inviolate, and those who would try to climb the heights any other way would surely find themselves in great trouble and, at the end of their effort, disappointed.

Repose is the greatest health-producing property of Matter, and he who acquires it will also acquire wisdom that cannot be obtained by the most intensive manipulation of material effects. This wisdom will dictate his every action and reaction, and will in time give him an unerring faculty of selection that nothing will enter his life that can in any way mar its functioning or disturb its poise. Quarrels can never come to those who have found their center of repose, for they have, in advance, met and conquered all the disturbing elemental differences.

Count that friend the most valuable whose demeanor is always one of calmness and repose. He has conquered the lions of irritability, anger, impatience, terror, fear, doubt and many others that are weeds of discordance in, alas, too many lives. He is the friend who can give the best advice who has already conquered himself and given the world an example of mastership in his life.

Let us, by purposeful repose, control our surroundings, making of every wind only a beautiful breeze to carry our barque further and further toward the glories of illumination and surcease from these ambassadors of unhappiness and discontent. When we have found our true center of repose the most difficult condition will fade away like the morning mist and the ministering angels of peace, happiness and love will fold us in their wings of light, and our hearts will rebound with the song of eternal morning where the Sun of Righteousness will encompass us round about and our eyes will have seen eternal glories.

True repose is found only on the Mount of Renunciation. There, above the restless surging and striving, the neophyte perceives his own soul and the illuminating light of supernal glory descends and surrounds him, blotting out the realms of sense and carrying him into the vales of contentment and peace. Renunciation means the lifting of the attention from the lower to the higher, from the coarser vibration to rarer and attenuated realms of Spirit, but the sense of rest and peace that surges through the spirit when the soul transcends the magnetic vibratory rating of the material and floats into the regions of Spirit so overcome with ecstacy that it is not given mortals words or poems to convey, or songs to illumine.

To sing the Song Sublime is to transcend the realms of sense, open the window of the soul, still the racing vibration of material senses, and open the eyes of the soul upon the Light of Eternal Truth. Only through the stillness of sweet repose can these faculties function and the glories of the Everlasting Light burst on the consciousness, illuming all Life and Truth.

Seek true repose and your center-of-being will find its recompense for its long exile in the realms of darkness, leaving it but a memory as a troubled dream.

—G.W.W.

POWER

Man's six powers are synthesized in the seventh. Each has seven subsidiary centers. Each has a positive and negative aspect. The seven are:

1. The Supreme Power — <u>Breath</u>. Breathe in Divine Love and Spiritual Power, breathe out health and love.

2. The power of Intellect — <u>Mind</u>. In man mind manifests in a three-fold way — subconscious or animal, conscious or human, super-conscious or divine — the Higher Self or Father-in-heaven.

3. The power of <u>Will</u> — free choice.

4. The power of <u>Thought</u> — imagination, etc.

5. The power of the <u>Life Principle</u> — control of nature, rhythm, overcoming fear, and the garden of peace. All this is possible for man.

6. The power of <u>Speech</u> — one of the greatest, the first power for man to master. (Each word is recorded on the Akashic Records.)

7. The power of becoming one in <u>Consciousness of God's Love.</u> Visualize God as Love, operating in this seven-fold Path of Power. Breathe it, visualize it, think it, will it, grasp it.

—M.D.W.

VIBRATION

Vibration is the movement of energy passing through substance. Its movement creates sound transmitted to consciousness at the level of its attention and awareness, enlightenment and degree of refinement or sensitivity.

Ideas create thought forms, thought forms create pictures. The wavelength of frequency determines substance, sound, color and form.

The frequency of energy in substance determines its density and volume. Hence, vibration is part of man's consciousness at every level of his awareness and growth. An unending outreach of his desire to interpret the universe and all that it reveals to him physically, mentally, emotionally, spiritually.

—M.B.W.

AURA

The auric body is a flashing vehicle of delicate hues. Thought forms appear in this radiant overcoat and they are seen by the reader. They appear as lucent shapes each influential with its specific energy.

Whether you retain a complete memory of your auric experience or have no recollection at all, your auric viewing, through its channel, will give you the development you need. Of course it is more enjoyable to your mind if you can be conscious of what you see and hear. You must understand <u>who you are, what you are</u> to do this. When this sky blue appears on the right of the auric passage <u>you can expect understanding.</u>

—from comments by Mary on an auric viewing

TEACHING BY MARY

<u>Spiritual Body</u> — The garment of the soul, used now (while living here) as body vehicle for the soul when it leaves the physical body in sleep. It is a consciousness put on by the soul as it leaves the physical body, and it dwells in the heaven world when not in use in invisible form. For one who has become a master of the law and forces of the universe, this spiritual body of his can be brought to him through the raising of vibrations and the desire of the soul, and thus clothing the soul or entity, it makes possible the going anywhere of that "person" in service as a disciple of the Christ and Master of development. This spiritual body is universal. Each soul has its own but its beauty and development are achieved by the living of a life of selflessness, in accord with the fundamental laws of love given us by the Christ's life and teaching. Events, emotions, thought and all else can be raised to the level of the consciousness of this spirit or highest self.

<u>The Three Bodies and Emotions or Desire</u> — There can develop a perfect balance among these three bodies which man possesses (physical, mental, spiritual). The mental, or thought one, maintains equilibrium, or balance, in the emotional realm, between the physical and the spiritual, so that one can remain on the ray of power. Raising emotion (including love) to this third or highest body brings a peace, adjustment to life's trials and tests, and also brings spiritual growth. Training through a teacher, knowledge gained in night work, intimate caring and help given by one's guides, and the "channel of divine power" are the priceless gifts to balanced control of the emotional bodies.

<u>The Soul</u> — There is in each person a white light which is "the light of the soul". To be conscious of our soul is to feel joy. The spirit is the active element of the soul. The soul gathers around itself elements which make it individual. It's the power of love which gives us this teaching. One far enough advanced can see this light, or the Holy Breath of Spirit. The soul leaves the body through the top of the head.

<u>Colors of Emotional Bodies</u> — There is a spectrum of color which in the physical desire body is strong, in the mental body less so and in the spiritual aura (above the head) still more delicate in shades. These colors change with the waves of emotion and thought given haven by the individual.

<u>Creative Thought</u> which flows or follows in a pattern, or in accord with the rays of force which the power of creative love sets in motion automatically, not only holds a soul in the realm of the positive love-force but makes that soul a co-creator with God in His work of creativity.

<u>The Seed of the Soul</u> — At the center of his being man contains all the colors of the spectrum like a chrysalis of color. The potential of perfection is contained therein, the seed or divine substance of his soul.

—M.D.W.

THE HEAVENLY WAY

The Heavenly Way is a Mystic Way
And the Mystic Way seems a strange way.

It is hidden and yet not hidden;
It is open and not open;
It is dark and yet not dark.

A strange way is this Mystic Way—
And more strange without a guide.
—Mary D. Weddell

    Christ's Love leads thee through mysterious doors. He is thy guide and friend. Trust His Love with all thy heart. When he sets thy feet upon His Path, the torch of Faith He will hand thee, and with it the staff of endurance. When thou art thus equipped and set forth on this Mystic Road, the hidden will be disclosed before the torch of Faith, and know it, "The Path".
—M.D.W.

GLOSSARY

Arc — A rainbow-shaped fan of twelve color rays with one dominant color. For example, the twelve rays of green in the Psychological Arc of Green, the twelve rays of red in the Spiritual Arc of Red, etc.

Aura — The radiation of God's light in the soul. All that man is — physical, mental-emotional and spiritual — is registered there.

Auric Viewing — A term used synonymously with color meditation. It involves the individual's getting quiet, raising his consciousness by whatever means most feasible, and then putting on paper the colors he sees or senses during this period of quiet.

Block — A rectangle of color used in color plumes.

Bridge — When making color plumes there is often the need to make a transition from one color to another. An intermediary color in smaller amount (about one-fourth the size of a block of color) is made between two blocks of color. This is to give smooth-flowing rhythm to the flow of the colors, an uplift like a half-note in music or the riser on a stairway.

Color — Term used for pure color, the hue of the color. When capitalized, Creative Color Analysis.

Color ray — A ray of light; the visible essence of an attribute or condition pertaining to the human aura.

Color, overtone — Made by applying a tint, shade or tone over a hue so that the hue shows through the overtone. It is to modify, brighten, lighten or deepen the hue's value — thereby creating expansion of meaning and relative value.

Channel — The Inner Channel is a spiralled etheric substance beginning at the solar plexus and reaching to the crown of the head, containing twelve specific colors. It is also called the Keys to the Kingdom since this inner portion of a human being is the path of light leading his consciousness to higher realms of understanding.

Mid-ray — A color dividing the ray and giving support to its two sides. The mid-ray often is the "feeding" portion giving strength to the balancing sides. The two sides can also support the mid-ray. Coded often MR.

Overlay — A color lightly applied over a color or colors.

Plume — A color prayer or visual affirmation. A sequence of color rays in the form of a column, usually a series of six blocks and five bridges which flow harmoniously. The colors are used to heal or transform a condition in oneself or others. It is used in meditation and/or as a visual affirmation combined with words. Color and sound combined create the most powerful color prayer.

Sandwiching — Lightly applying color by laying on the strokes first in one direction, then in the opposite direction and then over again in the same direction as the first strokes. This helps to blend the hues without changing the essence of the color.

Streaking — A process of lightly applying strokes of one or more colors over the basic foundational color when reproducing color rays with pastel chalks. Streaks can add meaning when applied from the right side and diminished toward the left or when applied from the bottom and diminished toward the top.

Striated — See streaking.

Striped — See streaking.

Swirl — A clockwise spiralled circular portion of color at the top of a plume, the mixed essences of colors in the plume. The action of the swirl creates the vibratory activity that sends it forth to heal, cleanse or nurture. The swirl is the sum total of the plume and contains the creative energy for which the plume was made. It also keeps the power within the plume.

Visual affirmation — See auric viewing and plume.

GUIDE TO COLOR DESCRIPTIONS OF THE RAYS

Abbreviations

Ps — Located in the Psychological Arc of the designated letter.

6B — A number plus a letter indicates a ray within the Spiritual Arc of the designated letter.

For example — Brown PsB, PsY, 5Y indicates the color is in the Psychological Arcs of Blue and Yellow and in the 5th Ray of the Spiritual Arc of Yellow.

Blue Green PsG (2), 8B is in two colors of the Psychological Arc of Green as well as in the 8th Ray of the Spiritual Arc of Blue.

G—Green   B—Blue   Y—Yellow   R—Red   P—Purple

Apricot
  clouded PsG
  pink PsG, 9Y

Bisque, rose 11P
Blue PsG, PsB, 3G, 9G
  bright PsB, 3B
    deep PsB
    light PsB
  cobalt 4B
    grayed PsB
  Copenhagen 5B
  dark PsB, 2B
    very 1B
  gray
    ashen PsB
    touch of 6B
  green
    deep PsB
    light Ps B
  light 9R
    soft PsB, 11G
  opaline 10B
  royal PsB
    bright PsB
  sky PsB, 11B
    irridescent, light 12B
    turquoise, light 9B
  Wedgewood 4B
Brown PsB, PsY, 5Y
  dark PsY
  gray, dullish 1G

  henna PsY
  pale PsY
  soft PsY
    streak of 5R
Buff 3Y

Chartreuse PsB, PsG
Copper, rosy PsY
Coral PsG, PsY
  orange PsR
  pale PsY
Coral Pink 6R

Flame, bit of 2Y
Flesh 10Y
Fuchia, rose, brilliant 7P

Gray
  blue, light 6B
  soft 1P
Green
  apple 9G
  blue PsG (2), 8B
  light PsB
  dark PsG, PsY, 1G
  deep PsG
  emerald, blue-tinted 6G
  forest, dark 3G
  grass 4G
  gray PsG (3), PsY

— 171 —

dark PsY
yellow, medium PsY
leaf, bright PsB
moss 8G
murky PsG
olive PsY, PsR
   dark 2G
   grayed PsR
   silvered 7G
orange, muddy PsR
seafoam 10G
soft 3R
yellow PsG (2)
   delicate 12G
   grayed PsG
   light PsG, 11G, 3Y
   soft PsG

Jade, green-blue, deep 7B

Lavender PsG, PsB
  blue 1P
    cobalt PsB
    light PsB
  gray, soft 1P
    light PsB
  pink, grayed 8P
  rose PsB
    rich PsR
Lilac, rose, soft 6P

Maroon PsB, 4R
Mustard, brown 1Y

Ochre, yellow
  dirtied PsY
  golden 2Y
Orange PsG, PsY (2), PsR, 1G, 2R
  dirty PsR (2)
  henna, dark 2G
  pale PsR

pink, light PsY
red PsR
  soft PsR
rose 1R
strong PsY (2)
yellow 7Y
Orchid
  blush 12P
  pink 5Y

Peach, rose 9P
Pink 11R
  apricot 9Y
  coral 6R
  flame 12Y
  flesh PsR (2), 10R
  peach 8Y
  rose PsR, 1P
  salmon PsY, 7R
    light PsR
    rosy PsR
Plum 8R
  blue 8R
  red 3P
Purple PsR, 1B, 4R
  rose 4P
  royal 2P

Red 2B, 4R, 8R
  bright PsR (2)
  deep 5R
  maroon PsR
  rose 5R, 6R
    rich PsR
    soft 3R
Rose PsB (2), 7Y
  coral 10R
  deep 5Y, 10Y, 7R
  lavender, deep PsR
  light 9R
  old 5G, 7G
    grayed, soft 12R
  pastel 7Y
  pink PsR
  red, light PsG

Scarlet 2R
Sienna, burnt PsY

Tangerine 5Y

White, blue, silvery 6Y

Yellow 6B, 8B, 12Y, 4R, 8R
  bright PsY, PsR
  canary 4Y
  green 5G
  light PsB, PsY (2)
  orange, light 1R
  pale 5Y, 7Y
  rich PsY (2)
  soft 3R
  sun, rich 11Y

GUIDE TO MEANINGS OF THE COLOR RAYS

Abbreviations

Ch — Located in The Inner Channel.

Ps — Located in the Psychological Arc of the designated letter. Psychological rays are usually referred to by their meanings such as "Joy," "Courage," etc.

10Y — A number plus a letter indicates a ray within the Spiritual Arc of the designated letter. Spiritual rays are most often referred to by number. For example, "Fourth of Blue" (4B) or "Tenth of Yellow" (10Y).

G—Green   B—Blue   Y—Yellow   R—Red   P—Purple

Able to judge truly   10Y
Acceptance of life's challenges   4G
Accomplishment, joy of   11G
Accountability   PsG
Accumulation   3Y
Act of at-one-ment with self   11G
Action of maturity   11Y
Active realization of good   3B
Adjustment to life   PsG
Age of Soul   7G
Aggression   PsR
Alert   10G
Ambition   PsB
Anger   PsR
Anger, derivatives of   2R
Anger, quick   2R
Appreciation   PsY
Asking forgiveness   5Y
Aspiration   1P
Assertion   PsR, 1G, 1Y
At-one-ment with God   12G
At-one-ment with Self   11G
Attained, much still to be, in life   1B
Attained, truth of self   9B
Attenuated, the Silver Cord   6Y
Aura, color at base of   1G
Aura, source of supply to   7Y
Aura, the ray one looks for first in reading an   7Y
Auras, a living ray, permanent, seen in all   6Y
Auras, reader of   11B, 7Y, 8G
Awareness, conscious   3B
Awareness of sowing and reaping   10G

Balance, foundational   3G
Balance, spiritual, Arc of Purple,   10B
Balanced enthusiasm   8R
Band of Teachers, holding force for Channel
Basic understanding   PsG
Benevolent at times   1Y
Bespeaks a soul seeking   7R
Best of things, talent for making   10R
Bigotry, has overcome   9R
Bodies, three, merging of   3R
Body, out of, the Silver Cord attenuated when   6Y
Born, twice   4R
Broken many habits, has   10Y
Broken old molds of thinking, has   10Y
Brother, tenderness and concern for   11R
Brotherhood   Channel

Capacity for loving   10Y
Carries his load willingly, happy and content   8R
Centered, Christ, life   9R
Challenge of life   1B
Challenges, acceptance of life's   4G
Charity   6P
Christ centered life   9R
Christ Jesus, shows one on Path of   4R
Christ, learning of, following cleansing   5R
Christ's Way, the struggle of 40 days in the wilderness, viewing the emotions   5R

Christ Within, nebulous ideas
  synchronized into a force unifying
  one with   11Y
Church and cult, This soul has sought
  through   11Y
Cleansing, deep   5R
Clear, Path made, through
  self-control   12G
Clear thinking and pure purpose   6R
Common sense   PsY
Compensation, the law of   10G
Comprehension, capable of spiritual   2B
Concept of life, a universal   12R
Concern, tenderness and, for a
  brother   11R
Confidence, steadfast   PsY
Confusion, less   9B
Conscious awareness of talents and source
  of power   3B
Conscious need of victory   7B
Conscious of immaturity   9G
Conscious understanding,
  expanding in   10G
Consciously identified with spiritual
  principles, life   4Y
Consciousness, entering higher   5G
Consciousness, fourth dimensional   12B
Consciousness of the oneness of the visible
  and invisible worlds   12B
Considerate and thoughtful of the needs
  of others   10R
Content, happy and   8R
Control emotion, power to   4B
Conversion, ray of   5R
Converts nature to spiritual expression
  toward fellow man   11Y
Cord, the Silver   6Y
Corrected, loathes to be   2Y
Courage, heroic   PsR
Courage, moral   PsB
Cowardice   PsY
Creation, seeing God in all   12R
Creative expression, recognizing the
  One Source in manifold form and
  color and degree of   12R
Creative Life Force   PsR
Criticism   2R
Cult, This soul has sought through many
  channels of church and   11Y

Death, The Silver Cord severed
  only at   6Y
Deceit   PsY
Decisions, spiritual   9B
Deep cleansing   5R
Degree of (spiritual) development
  attained   7Y
Denotes ego   7B
Depth of Love   3P
Derivatives of anger   2R
Desire   PsY
Desire, no, to star   11R
Desire to do something about truth of self
  revealed in wilderness   5R
Desire to share   7R
Desirelessness   Channel
Determination to follow the spiritual
  way   8R
Developed, a type easily   9Y
Developed person, a God Ray of a   12Y
Developing on the Path, shows one   9R
Development, has great power for   7R
Development, spiritual, degree attained
  of, shown by location of ray   7Y
Development (spiritual), hidden   8G
Development, spiritual, shown by
  color   7Y
Discernment   10B
Disinterest in general   1G
Divine force beautifies   8B
Divine imagination   4P
Doling out sparingly   3Y
Dominating   1Y
Domination modified   1Y
Dreams and visions will begin to be
  comprehended   6R
Duties, duty, see "Load"

Earnestly trying   4Y
Ego, denotes   7B
Ego, subduing the   8B
Ego, Training of, Basic Auric Rays,
  Arc of Blue
Ego, transforming the power of   8B
Emotion   PsB
Emotion, power to control   4B
Emotional force   5B
Emotions, viewing in wilderness   5R

Endeavoring to keep integrated by
   Spirit   4Y
Energy directed Godward   8R
Enlightenment   Channel
Entering higher consciousness   5G
Enthusiasm, balanced   8R
Evil intent   PsB
Exaggeration   2R
Exaggeration, speaks truth without   3R
Expanding in conscious
   understanding   10G

Fairminded   3G
Faith   Channel, 2P
Faith, testing ground of   1R
Fall, less prone to   6B
Fear   PsB
Feeling rather than reason   5B
Fellow man (see also "All men",
   "Mankind" "Brother")   11Y
Field of realization and overcoming   1R
Follow a leader, keen to   8Y
Follow the Spiritual Way,
   determination to   8R
Force beautifies, Divine   8B
Force, emotional   5B
Force for Teachers, Holding   Channel
Force, Holding . . . emotion   4B
Force, life, expressed by spirit   3R
Force, life, stabilized   6B
Force of patience, Holding   Channel
Force unifying oneself with the Christ
   within, a   11Y
Force, vibrant universal   5G
Forces, higher, entering the path   4R
Forgiveness, asking   5Y
Form and color, recognizing the
   One Source in manifold   12R
Forty days, struggle of   5R
Foundational balance   3G
Fourth dimensional consciousness   12B
Friendship   PsR
Fundamental righteousness   2G

Generosity   PsG
Glorification, self-   2R
God, at-one-ment with   12G

God in all creation, seeing   12R
God Ray of a developed person, a   12Y
Godward, energy directed   8R
Gold about a person   12Y
Good, active realization of   3B
Gossip   PsY
Grace   11P,   Channel
Gratitude   9P
Greed   PsR
Growth, Basic Auric Rays, Arc of Green
Growth, new   PsG
Growth, Realization of   9B

Habits, has broken many   10Y
Habits of the past, man faced by   5Y
Happiness   PsY
Happy and content   8R
Harmony   8P
Harmony, Life's   PsB
Hatred   PsR
Hearing, spiritual, and sight   10B
Heavenly realms   12B
Heavenly teacher, drawn to   12B
Heroic courage   PsR
Hidden (spiritual) development   8G
Higher consciousness, entering   5G
Higher forces entering the path   4R
Holding force, power to control
   emotion   4B
Holding force for the Band of Teachers
   Channel
Holding force of Patience   Channel
Honesty   PsG
Honor   PsR

Ideas synchronized   11Y
Illumination, Basic Auric Rays,
   Arc of Yellow
Illumination   12G
Illumination, supply of, to the aura   7Y
Imagination, discernment
   concerning   10B
Imagination, Divine   4P
Immaturity, conscious of   9G
Indifference   PsG
Indifference to spiritual
   development   1G

Innate refinement   PsB
Inspiration   Channel
Integrated by Spirit, endeavoring to keep   4Y
Integration of spiritual powers   10B
Integrity   PsG
Intellect   PsY
Invisible and visible worlds, consciousness of   12B

Jealousy   PsG
Jesus, see Christ
Joy   PsR
Joy of accomplishment   11G
Judge truly, able to   10Y
Judge self truly, has learned to   10Y
Justice   PsB
Justification, self-   2R

Keen to follow a leader   8Y
Keys to the Kingdom   Channel
Kindly and often self-sacrificing   8Y
Kindness, virtues of   10R
Knowledge, standing on premise of having all   2Y

Law of compensation   10G
Lay down the "old man", willing to   4R
Leader, keen to follow a   8Y
Learned to judge self truly   10Y
Learning of Him   5R
Less confusion   9B
Less prone to fall   6B
Life, adjustment to   Ps G
Life, challenge of   1B
Life, Christ centered   9R
Life consciously identified   4Y
Life force, creative   PsR
Life force stabilized   6B
Life force expressed by spirit   3R
Life, love of   9Y
Life, reality of   4G
Life, spiritual   11B
Life, spiritual, present in the physical   6G
Life, testing ground of   1B
Life, universal concept of   12R

Life's challenges, acceptance of   4G
Life's harmony   PsB
Living ray, a (the Silver Cord)   6Y
Load, carries his, willingly   8R
Loathes to be corrected   2Y
Longing   1P
Love, (mental-emotional)   PsR
Love, depth of   3P
Love, human   PsR
Love of life, a soul naturally filled with   9Y
Love of mankind   9Y
Love, walks the way of, tempered by Spirit   10Y
Loving, capacity for   10Y
Loyalty   PsB
Lust   PsR

Man as a spiritual being   12B
Man faced by habits of the past   5Y
Man must overcome, the steep and rugged path   5Y
Mankind, love of   9Y
Maturing action   11Y
Maturity, action of   11Y
Measure of peace, a   11G
Men, he respects himself and all   10Y
Mental body   3R
Mental or spiritual opinions strong   9G
Mental-emotional love (human)   PsR
Mental peace   PsY
Merging of three bodies   3R
Message bearer   Channel
Message, reality of   10B
Metamorphosis, Basic auric rays of Arc of Red
Mind and spirit, union of,   Channel
Minded, fair-   3G
Molds of thinking, has broken old   10Y
Moral courage   PsB
Motivation   PsY

Natural Ray for accumulation   3Y
Naturally filled, a soul   9Y
Nature, a, resplendent in warmth and virtues of kindness   10R
Nature, a warm   8Y

Nature, converts, to spiritual expression toward fellow man   11Y
Nebulous ideas synchronized   11Y
New growth   PsG
New, ready for   4R
Night teaching   12B
No waste of power   4B

Old in experience, a soul   2Y
"Old man", willing to lay down the   4R
Old molds of thinking, has broken   10Y
Old soul   2B
Older soul . . . more rose   6G
Opinion, pride of   2R
Opinion, strong   1Y
Opinions, strong, mental or spiritual   9G
Opinions, stubborn   2G
Orb, within ray   7Y
Others, considerate of needs of   10R
Others may shine, steps in the shade that   11R
Overcome bigotry, has   9R
Overcome, the steep and rugged path man must   5Y
Overcoming, field of   1R
Over-confident   2Y

Past, man faced by habits of   5Y
Path, higher forces entering the   4R
Path made clear through self-control   12G
Path of Christ Jesus, shows one on   4R
Path, the steep and rugged, man must overcome   5Y
Patience, holding force of   Channel
Peace   Channel   10P
Peace, a measure of   11G
Peace, mental   PsY
Permanent, a living ray . . . Silver Cord   6Y
Perseverance   7R
Philanthropy   PsG
Physical body merging with mental and spiritual   3R
Physical, Spiritual life present in the   6G
Poise   3G
Positive stand   3B
Potential power   1R

Power, conscious awareness of source of   3B
Power for development, great   7R
Power, no waste of   4B
Power of the ego, transforming the   8B
Power, potential   1R
Power to control emotion   4B
Powers, spiritual, integration of   10B
Prayer life ray. See "spiritual life"   11B
Prayers, selfless   11B
Premise of having all knowledge   2Y
Pride   PsR
Pride of opinion   2R
Principles, spiritual   4Y
Promise of spiritual sight   6R
Prophecy   Channel
Purpose, pure   6R

Quest of Spirit, reveals man is on   5Y
Quick anger   2R

Ray, a living   6Y
Ray, a natural, for accumulation   3Y
Ray of conversion   5R
Ray, first, of wisdom   6R
Ray seen in all auras   6Y
Ray reveals source of supply to the Aura   7Y
Ready for the "new"   4R
Reality of life   4G
Reality of message   10B
Realization of good, active   3B
Realization, field of   1R
Realization of growth   9B
Realization of man as a spiritual being   12B
Reaping, awareness of sowing and   10G
Reason, feeling rather than   5B
Rebirth, shows   5Y
Rebirth, sign of   6G
Rebuilding, necessity for   5B
Receptive   10G
Refinement needed   1B
Reliability   PsB
Respects self and all men   10Y
Responsibility   PsB
Responsibility taken   11G

Reveals man is on quest of Spirit   5Y
Revelation of truth, discernment concerning   10B
Revelation, self-   1P
Righteousness, fundamental   2G
Rugged path, the steep and, man must overcome   5Y

Scandal   PsY
Seeing God in all creation   12R
Seeking, bespeaks a soul   7R
Self-analysis   PsB
Self-asserting   1Y
Self-assertion   1G
Self, at-one-ment with   10G
Self-centered   2G
Self-control, path made clear through   12G
Self, drawing all things to the   3Y
Self-glorification   2R
Self-respect   10Y
Self-revelation   1P
Self-sacrificing, kindly   8Y
Self, truth of, attained   9B
Self, truth of, revealed   5R
Selfless prayers   11B
Selflessness   9R
Sense, common   PsY
Serenity   Channel, 12P
Set, very   1Y
Severed only at death, the Silver Cord   6Y
Shade, steps in, that others may shine   11R
Share, desire to   7R
Shock through fear   PsG
Shows one on the Path of Christ Jesus   4R
Shows rebirth   5Y
Sight and hearing, spiritual   10B
Sight, spiritual, promise of   6R
Sign of rebirth   6G
Sign to the teacher. . .8G
Silver Cord, the   6Y
Sloth   1G
Soul, age of   7G
Soul naturally filled with the love of life, of mankind, a   9Y

Soul has sought through many channels   11Y
Soul, old   2B
Soul old in experience   2Y
Soul seeking   7R
Soul urge, great   7B
Source of light to the aura   7Y
Source of power, conscious awareness of   3B
Source, recognizing the one, in manifold form and color   12R
Sowing and reaping, awareness of   10G
Sparingly, doling out   3Y
Speaks truth without exaggeration   3R
Spirit, endeavoring to keep integrated by   4Y
Spirit, life force expressed by   3R
Spirit, reveals man is on quest of   5Y
Spirit, the way of love tempered by   10Y
Spirit, union of mind and,   Channel
Spiritual balance, Basic Auric Rays, Arc of Purple,   10B
Spiritual being, man as   12B
Spiritual body merging with physical and mental   3R
Spiritual comprehension, capable of   2B
Spiritual decisions more quickly made   9B
Spiritual development of a person   7Y
Spiritual life   11B
Spiritual life present in the physical   6G
Spiritual opinions strong, mental or   9G
Spiritual powers, integration of   10B
Spiritual principles, life consciously identified with   4Y
Spiritual sight and hearing   10B
Spiritual sight, promise of   6R
Spiritual Voice   Channel
Spiritual wisdom   5P
Stability   3G
Stabilized, life force   6B
Stand, positive   3B
Star, no desire to   11R
Steadfast confidence   PsY
Steep and rugged path man must overcome, the   5Y
Steps in the shade that others may shine   11R
Strong opinion   1Y
Strong opinions, mental or spiritual   9G

Struggle of 40 days in the wilderness 5R
Stubborn opinions 2G
Student has hidden development 8G
Subduing the ego to some extent 8B
Supply PsG
Supply of light or illumination to the aura, source of 7Y
Sympathetic Understanding 7P

Talent for making the best of things 10R
Talents, conscious awareness of 3B
Teacher, could become a 7R
Teacher, heavenly 12B
Teacher, sign to the 8G
Teachers, good 1Y
Teaching, night, in higher heavenly realms 12B
Temperate in all things 10Y
Tempered by Spirit, walks the way of love 10Y
Tenderness and concern for a brother 11R
Tested, often 2Y
Testing ground of faith 1R
Testing ground of life 1B
Things, doling out sparingly 3Y
Thinking, clear, and pure purpose 6R
Thinking, has broken old molds of 10Y
Thoughtful of needs of others, considerate and 10R
Three bodies, mental, physical and spiritual 3R
Tolerant with understanding 12R
Tone of life beautified and modified 8B
Training of the Ego, Basic Auric Rays, Arc of Blue
Transforming the power of the ego 8B
Truth, discernment concerning 10B
Truth of self attained 9B
Truth of self revealed 5R
Trying, earnestly 4Y
Twice born, 4R, see also "Rebirth"
Type easily developed, a 9Y

Understanding, basic PsG
Understanding, expanding in conscious 10G
Understanding, tolerant with 12R

Unifying oneself with the Christ Within 11Y
Union of mind and spirit Channel
Universal concept of life, a 12R
Universal force, a vibrant 5G
Urge, great soul 7B

Vibrant universal force 5G
Victory, conscious need of 7B
Visible and invisible worlds, oneness of 12B
Visions and dreams, comprehension of 6R
Voice, spiritual Channel

Walks the way of Love, tempered by Spirit 10Y
Warm nature, a 8Y
Warmth and kindness, nature resplendent in 10R
Waste of power, no 4B
Way, Christ's 5R
Way of Love tempered by Spirit, walks the 10Y
Wilderness, forty days struggle in 5R
Will to do 6B
Willing to lay down the "old man," ready for the new 4R
Willingly, carries his load 8R
Wisdom, first ray of 6R
Widsom, spiritual 5P
Wise, at times 1Y
World, oneness of visible and invisible 12B

Yearning 1P

Zealous 2G